Current Topics in Early Childhood Education

Volume VII

Editor
LILIAN G. KATZ

Associate Editor
Karen Steiner

ERIC *Clearinghouse on Elementary and Early Childhood Education, University of Illinois at Urbana-Champaign*

ABLEX PUBLISHING CORPORATION
Norwood, New Jersey 07648

Printed in the United States of America

Office of Educational
Research and Improvement
U.S. Department of Education

This publication was prepared with funding from the Office
of Educational Research and Improvement, U.S. Department of Education, under contract no. OERI 400-83-0021.
The opinions expressed in this report do not necessarily reflect the positions or policies of OERI or the Department of
Education.

ISBN 0-89391-407-X (C)
ISBN 0-89391 416-9 (P)   ISSN 0363-8332

Ablex Publishing Corporation
355 Chestnut Street
Norwood, New Jersey 07648

Contents

5 **Motivation and School Achievement**
Martin L. Maehr and Jennifer Archer... **85**

6 **Toward an Interactional Model of Developmental Changes
in Social Pretend Play**
Artin Göncü.. **108**

7 **Children's Humor: A Cognitive-Developmental Perspective**
Amelia J. Klein... **126**

Acknowledgments

The editors are greatly indebted to Millie Almy, Carole Ames, Rhoda McShane Becher, Libby Byers, Greta Fein, Susan Harter, Gwen Morgan, Sherri Oden, Donald L. Peters, James Raths, Bernard Spodek, Brian Sutton–Smith, and C. Ray Williams for their careful reviews and thoughtful comments on the papers in this volume.

Preface

The first volume in this series on current topics in early childhood education was published in 1977. We bring you this last one with mixed emotions: sorrow at seeing the series go but pleasure at welcoming its replacement, the *Early Childhood Research Quarterly,* also published by Ablex Publishing Corporation. As we take stock of what has been offered through the seven-volume series, we are pleased to note that 92 of the leading scholars in the field of early childhood education have presented their ideas in *Current Topics* and seven of these authors have included their work in more than one volume. We also note that six authors are from Australia, three from Canada, two each from Britain and West Germany, and one from Ireland. We hope international participation will continue and grow in the *Quarterly*.

Like those in previous volumes, the topics addressed in this one are diverse. The first chapter, on the nature of professions and the extent of professionalization of early childhood education, reflects growing concern over the standards of practice and status of workers in the field. One important aspect of a profession is the nature and content of its knowledge base. In the next chapter in the volume, Silin explores this topic and reveals some of the perplexing issues in it, especially as they relate to what teachers need to know and to teacher education.

Biemiller and his colleagues describe the variety of provisions for young children in Canada, the largest country in the world. Subsequently, Burton reviews the rich and growing research on the development of social competence, a topic addressed by Asher, Oden, and Gottman in Volume I and again by Oden in Volume IV. Maehr and Archer review the extensive literature on motivation, a subject discussed earlier by Condry and Koslowski in Volume II and by Deci and Ryan in Volume V. In his chapter on developmental changes and social pretend play, Göncü extends work in an area first explored by Fein in Volume II, Stern in Volume IV, and Almy and colleagues in Volume V. Finally, Klein presents a discussion of the interesting research on children's humor, a topic not addressed in previous volumes but one that we hope will be the subject of future investigation.

Once again, the variety of topics represented in this last volume of *Current Topics in Early Childhood Education* reflects the complexity of the field. We hope that the new journal, *Early Childhood Research Quarterly,* will continue to provide readers with a forum to publish their own works and to benefit from the work of colleagues.

Lilian G. Katz, Ph.D.
Director, ERIC Clearinghouse on Elementary
and Early Childhood Education

1

The Nature of Professions: Where Is Early Childhood Education?

Lilian G. Katz

University of Illinois at Urbana–Champaign

The purpose of this chapter is to apply some of the main features of the concept of a profession to the current state of the art of early childhood education. However, before launching into the discussion, I would like to indicate some of the bases for my interest in this topic.

There is at present a strong drive toward the professionalization of teaching in general and teaching and working in preschool settings in particular. With respect to the latter, the Illinois Association for the Education of Young Children has established the Illinois Society of Early Childhood Professionals, an organization open only to specially qualified members of the National Association for the Education of Young Children (NAEYC). The Illinois society is expected to be a model for adoption by other state groups interested in strengthening professionalism among early childhood educators and childcare workers.

The mounting pressure to identify and acknowledge early childhood "professionals" is in part due to grave concerns over the very low pay, status, and prestige of those who work in preschool settings. Indeed, the theme of the 1985 annual conference of NAEYC was "Early Childhood Education: A Proud Profession!" But this theme might be seen as a case of protesting too much. While early childhood workers may not be members of an "ashamed" profession, considering its public image, financial status, and intellectual standing (Silin, 1985), it can hardly be described as a "proud" one.

Another basis for my interest in the status of the early childhood practitioner is the assumption that we cannot have optimal environments for children unless the environments are also optimal for the adults who work with children. For several years, taking this assumption as virtually axiomatic, I have tried to describe the factors required to create optimal environments for teachers of young children (cf. Katz, 1977). By focusing on the needs of teachers, I do not intend in any way to diminish the centrality of parents' roles in their children's welfare and development. On the contrary, it seems to me that it is in the best interests of parents to be concerned about the qualities, status, and working conditions of their children's teachers and caregivers.

In other words, improving the lot of teachers is in no way antithetical to the interests of parents. Indeed, there is persuasive evidence that young children are very sensitive to the moods, emotional states, and morale of the adults around them (Cummings, Iannotti, & Zahn–Waxler, 1985). Thus, it seems useful to illuminate issues relating to those factors affecting the status and morale of teachers of young children. However, we must acknowledge that much of what is required to upgrade the conditions and wages of practitioners would place a heavy burden upon precisely that portion of the population that can least afford to accept it.

WHAT ARE THE CHARACTERISTICS OF A PROFESSION?

Early in this century, scholars began analyzing the nature of professions. Analyses continue apace today as more and more occupational groups strive to upgrade themselves to professional status (Forsyth & Danisiewicz, 1983; Goode, 1983). Many definitions of the term "professional" appear in the literature. While I have attempted to synthesize these various definitions, for the purpose of this discussion I am drawing most heavily on the work of H. S. Becker (1962) in his classic paper, "The Nature of a Profession."

Becker distinguishes between two uses of the term "professional": the scientific concept and the "folk" concept. The former refers to the way social scientists use the term, and the latter corresponds to meanings given to the term in everyday language.

Popular Uses of the Term "Profession"

According to Becker (1962), the folk conception of a profession is evaluative in that it is used as an honorific designation. In popular use, the term denotes a quality of spirit, an exceptional level of dedication to morally praiseworthy work. It is also associated with high social status and is often assumed to be correlated with a high income. As is apparent from the realities of the field of early professional education, much of the drive toward professionalization is based on popular rather than scientific connotations.

With respect to achieving the goals implicit in the popular conception of professionalism, early childhood practitioners do not seem to be doing very well. It is my impression from extensive experience with colleagues in many parts of the world that the younger the child with whom the practitioner works, the less training is required, the less ability is expected, the lower the pay, the fewer the working benefits, and the poorer the working conditions.

While it may seem to us that our moral praiseworthiness should be obvious to all, acknowledgment of this fact is not widespread. I think this situation is due in part to the possibility that, in many countries, people really believe that young children should be at home with their mothers enjoying what is sometimes referred to as a "Norman Rockwellian" version of family life. While the fact that young children participate in various kinds of preschool settings is not to be blamed on the workers who staff them, many laypeople believe that the work involved in caring for children is no more than minding babies whose mothers are otherwise engaged.

We ourselves have consistently and strongly asserted that young children learn through play. It is perhaps not surprising, then, to find policymakers and others suggesting that children might just as well be left to play at home or on the neighborhood playground. Such critics frequently assert that such learning experiences do not require the provision of highly trained personnel, specialized buildings, or equipment. However, contemporary research and scholarship concerning the role and effects of play on various aspects of development shows play to be a very complex phenomenon (cf. Brown & Gottfried, 1985; Carpenter, 1983). We must be careful to indicate that some play experiences are more beneficial than others and to stress that adults have a major role in maximizing the benefits children may derive from them.

As to our status, good reason exists to believe that, as the proportion of women in an occupation increases, its status decreases (Wolfle, 1978). As if that were not good enough, there is also evidence that the status of a practitioner is correlated with the status of the client. If this is indeed the case, then teachers and nannies who work with the offspring of high-status and high-income families may enjoy greater status than those who work with the children of inner-city poor or unemployed parents. Such status diffusion, applicable to many fields of work, is unlikely to be altered much by the present drive toward professionalism.

Scientific Definitions of the Term "Profession"

Most scholars of the subject agree that eight criteria must be met before a field of endeavor may be termed a profession. In the absence of a formal or conceptual rationale for ordering the importance of these criteria, I shall introduce them in order of those to be treated most briefly first and most fully last.

Social Necessity

Most scholars include as a criterion of a profession that the work must be essential to the functioning of a society, suggesting that the absence of its knowledge and techniques would weaken the society in some way.

The evidence bearing on whether or not the work of early childhood educators is essential to society is mixed at best. While recent reports of the longitudinal effects of early childhood education (Consortium for Longitudinal Studies, 1983) are very encouraging, they are in need of large-scale replication. We still have a long way to go to make a convincing case that teachers of the highest quality can provide services to young children without which society is at risk.

Given the power of experiences in later childhood and adolescence to offset the benefits of good early experiences, we must be very careful in the statements we make about what we can achieve. We can be no more sure that the effects of good early experiences cannot be reversed than that early bad experiences can be remediated. Haskins's (1985) recent report of a long term follow-up study of primary schoolchildren who had been in day care has indicated that such children are more aggressive in their primary school years than children not in day care and that those who had been in "cognitive" programs were more aggressive than those in other types of settings. Since we do not know what Haskins meant by "cognitive," these results are highly susceptible to misinterpretation and abuse by policymakers. Nor is it likely that any of the subjects in his study were in programs of the quality to which most of us are committed.

Altruism

The mission of a profession is said to be altruistic in that it is service-oriented rather than profit-oriented. Professionals are said to have clients rather than customers or consumers. Ideally, professionals are expected to perform their services with unselfish dedication, if necessary working beyond their normal hours and giving up personal comforts in the interests of society. Professions identify the goals of their work with the good of humanity at large, placing strong emphasis on social ends in contrast to the more tangible or immediate ends served by tradespeople, merchants, or entertainers.

On this criterion, we ought to be doing very well. No one can claim that teachers of young children are busy amassing riches or engaged in work that is simply easy or glamorous! The service ideal and client-centeredness of professions seems clearly characteristic of teaching in general and early childhood teaching in particular.

Autonomy

Most scholars in the sociology of professions agree that, ideally, a profession is an occupation that is autonomous in at least two ways (Forsyth & Danisiewicz, 1983). The client is autonomous in that he or she does not dictate to the practitioner what services are to be rendered or how they are to be received. Ideally, professionals who practice in large organizations or institutions are also autonomous with respect to their employer, who does not dictate the nature of practice but hires the professional to exercise judgment based on specialized knowledge, principles, and techniques. As Braude (cited in Forsyth & Danisiewicz, 1983) points out, "To the degree that a worker is constrained in the performance of his work by the controls and demands of others, that individual is less professional."

Issues concerning autonomy with respect to clients are complex for the early childhood educator. Our profession has at least three client groups: parents, children, and society or posterity. All of us are challenged by the paradoxical situation of wanting to strengthen and increase parent involvement in children's education while at the same time wishing to exercise our best professional judgment as to what is in children's best interests. We still have much to learn about how to be more sensitive to parents without being intimidated by them. To laypersons, parent involvement seems so simple that our apparent resistance to it is difficult to understand. A large part of the parent involvement problem is that parents are not a monolithic aggregate. Understandably, parents do not all agree on what goals and methods are appropriate for early childhood education.

Let us hope that we work in a country that prizes diversity of views, values, opinions, and cultures among the parents of the children we teach. However, the more diverse the client group, the less likely it is that all the parents of any one teacher's pupils will be equally satisfied. To which of the parents is the teacher to accede? All of them? The one with the loudest voice? The highest status? In the United States, schools have always been responsive to parents— but not to *all* parents — just to the one or two who have power and status in the community. To develop as a profession requires that we learn how to respond on the basis of our very best professional judgment, based on the best available knowledge and practices, to desires that are sometimes strident and often contradictory.

Although parents and society at large are served by our profession, most teachers think of children as their primary clients. A possible pitfall exists in this narrow view of the client group. Specifically, every "school of thought," educational method, or approach in part argues its merits on the basis that "the children love it." Maybe so. But the fact that children "love" an activity is not sufficient justification for its inclusion in the curriculum. Children love candy, junk food, silly cartoons, and what many of us consider inappropriate television programs. Although children's preferences must be taken into consideration, decisions concerning curriculum should not be made solely on the basis of the enjoyment of one client group. Enjoyment, in and of itself, is not an appropriate goal for education. The appropriate goal for education — at every level — is to engage the learner's mind and to assist that mind in its efforts to make better and deeper sense of significant experiences. I should add here that when teachers accomplish this end most children find their education enjoyable. In other words, enjoyment is a by-product rather than a goal of good teaching.

In a sense, society or posterity is the educator's ultimate client. But societies like ours often demand incompatible achievements. They want the young to learn to be both cooperative and competitive. They want conformity and initiative. It is no simple matter to help children learn where and when such different dispositions are appropriate. Our communities say that, at the least, they want excellence, high standards of achievement, and equality of opportunity. What principles of learning, development, curriculum, evaluation, and testing can we apply to meet such multiple and often contradictory expectations (cf. Green, 1983)?

Code of Ethics

Consistent with client-centeredness, professional societies subscribe to a code of ethics intended to protect the best interests of clients and to minimize yielding to the temptations inherent in the practice of the profession. In addition, professional societies institute procedures for disciplining members in cases of violations of the code of ethics.

The development of a code of ethics for early childhood educators is not an easy task. The process involves identifying the major temptations confronted in the course of practice (Katz, 1984c). The code should address ethical dilemmas inherent in relations with children, parents, colleagues, employers, and the public. Many people are skeptical about the usefulness of such codes. However, it seems to me that the ethical norms of a group of colleagues, articulated in a code of ethics, can help to give individual members the feeling that colleagues will back them up when they have to take a risky but courageous stand on a controversial ethical issue. It is likely that when we believe our fellow practitioners will take the same stands or would censure us if we failed to live up to our code, our commitment to right action is strengthened.

The NAEYC has formed a special committee to work on the development of a code for its members. Several state branches of the association have already developed their own. Inasmuch as local values and cultural variations play a strong role in the conception of ethical standards, it would seem wise for each country, region, or cultural unit to develop its own code.

Distance from Client

Since, by definition, the practice of a profession requires bringing to bear a body of knowledge and principles to the solution of problems and predicaments, the relationship between practitioner and client is marked by optimal emotional distance, disinterest, or "detached concern" (Katz, 1984a). This distance from the client is reflected in the taboo against physicians' treating members of their own families; in such situations, it is felt that emotional attachment and empathy might interfere with the exercise of reasoned judgment. This feature of professional practice does not preclude such feelings as empathy or compassion, but is intended to place these feelings in perspective. Emphasis on such optimal distance is also expected to minimize the temptation to develop favorites among children and parents, and to inhibit the tendency to respond to clients in terms of personal predilection or impulse rather than on the basis of reasoned judgment.

I am aware that many specialists and teachers in early childhood education resist the detachment aspect of professionalism—and not without reason. Among other things, they worry about meeting children's apparent need for closeness and affection. However, young children generally are capable of experiencing such feelings even when the teacher maintains an optimal distance. Though effective teaching requires intimate knowledge of pupils, this can be achieved by frequent contact, observation, and listening without the kind of emotionality required of family relationships. Many early childhood educators associate optimal distance with a stereotypical view of a remote, unresponsive, and intimidating expert who is likely to trigger resentment among parents. In fact, optimal distance serves to protect the teacher from the risks of "burnout" that can endanger performance and, therefore, effectiveness with children. I want to emphasize that the emotional distance should be an optimal one in that it permits the teacher to be responsive, caring, and compassionate, as well as to exercise professional judgment and bring knowledge to bear on responses to children.

Standards of Practice

Most scholars also agree that a profession adopts standards of practice that are significant in three ways:

1. Standards are adopted below which it is hoped no practitioner will fall. These standards are meant to ensure that every practitioner applies the standard procedures in the course of exercising professional judgment. In some measure, these standards result in the standardization of professional performance (e.g., all physicians follow standard procedures in making diagnoses but exercise their own judgment in deciding what actions to take). In theory, at least, professional practice is distinguished from the work of artisans, tradespeople, technicians, or bureaucrats in that it does not simply implement fixed routines, rules of

thumb, or regulations. Rather than following a set of prescriptions, the professional practitioner acts on the basis of accepted principles which are taken into account in the formulation of professional judgment.

2. Standards developed and adopted are addressed to the standard predicaments that every member can be expected to encounter fairly often in the course of practice. The standard procedures applied to the standard problems encountered in the course of practice are accumulated into the body of professional knowledge.

3. Standards of performance are universalistic rather than particularistic. Universalistic standards of performance imply that all the knowledge, skill, insight, ingenuity, etc., possessed by the practitioner is available to every client, independent of such irrelevant personal attributes of the client as social and ethnic background, ability to pay, or personal appeal.

One of the major tasks ahead for us, as I see it, is to develop and articulate our perceptions of professional standards. One approach that we might consider is to enumerate and describe the standard predicaments that all early childhood educators confront in the course of their day-to-day work. One such effort of my own (Katz, 1984b), depicts a situation in which 4-year-olds quarrel over whose turn it is to use a tricycle. In this examination, the responses of a professionally trained teacher are compared with the responses of an untrained person in order to highlight how professional judgment comes into play.

A colleague and I are now working on a paper concerning standard predicaments teachers of young children may encounter in their work with parents (Katz & Becher, 1985). We have identified five types of predicaments: (a) differences between a parent and a teacher concerning pedagogical issues; (b) parents' expectations for their own children that might undermine the welfare of other children in the group; (c) parental hostility, anger, or denial of a teacher's competence; (d) a teacher's need to inform a parent that his or her child's development is not going well and that special help is required; and (e) a teacher's perception that the parents' behavior puts the child's development at risk.

Our task is to suggest professionally appropriate responses for each of the five types of predicaments and to indicate what knowledge, principles, and professional techniques might be applied. Our hope is that this kind of effort will help in developing the body of knowledge, principles, and techniques that should underlie professional practice. Much more work needs to be done along these lines; such work requires identifying the most important predicaments and articulating our understanding of the knowledge and practices that can help in problem resolution.

Prolonged Training

Most scholars of the sociology of professions agree that a major defining attribute of a profession is that it requires entrants to undergo prolonged training. Although there are no standards by which to judge how long such training should be, the training process itself is thought to have several particular characteristics:

1. The training is specialized in order to ensure the acquisition of complex knowledge and techniques.
2. The training processes are difficult and require cognitive strain. As a consequence of careful screening, some candidates can be expected to fail. Training should be marked by optimal stress and sacrifice, resulting in dedication and commitment to the profession (Katz & Raths, 1986).
3. In all professions, candidates are required to master more knowledge than is likely to be applied and more than the student perceives to be necessary. In all professions, candidates complain about these excesses and the apparent irrelevance of much of the knowledge they are expected to master.
4. Institutions responsible for professional training must be accredited or licensed by processes monitored by practicing members of the profession. These institutions award certificates, diplomas, or degrees under the supervision of members of the profession.
5. All professional training institutions offer trainees a common core of knowledge and techniques so that the entire membership of the profession shares a common allusionary base.
6. Professional societies and training institutions, very often in concert, provide systematic and regular continuing education for members.

It is not clear what kind and amount of training is required for high-quality professional performance (see, for example, Katz, 1984b). In general, I think we should stop being defensive about expecting candidates in teacher education to study theory, research, history, and philosophy. My reasons for this stance include the point made above that all professions expose their candidates to more knowledge than they ever apply, expecting not more than about a third of what is mastered to be retained. (The more studied, the larger that third is.). Furthermore, evidence exists to show that, even though one forgets facts and concepts once mastered, such knowledge enables one to go on absorbing new facts and concepts more easily long after training has been completed (Broudy, 1983). In addition, I would like to suggest that there is a sense in which it is important for practitioners to be "literate" in their own fields: Though they may never use Montessori's ideas, all early childhood practitioners should know who she was and should comprehend the main ideas she espoused.

In many countries, there is cause for concern about the characteristics of entrants into training. Too often, young women are advised to enter early childhood education because their shyness makes them unsuitable for work with older pupils or because they are not academically strong enough to take up a more challenging or profitable occupation. Sadly, we have heard reports from several countries that preschool teachers have been urged to transfer into secondary teaching because they were judged "too good for infants."

Disheartening evidence exists to suggest that, among graduates of teacher education degree programs, those with the greatest ability last the shortest length of time in the teaching service (Schlecty & Vance, 1981). As more alternatives and attractive opportunities for women become available, this "brain drain" is likely to continue. It can only be stemmed if working conditions and pay are dramatically improved and if the needs of young children are given higher social priority. To some extent, the field of early childhood education—especially child care and day nursery work—is caught in a vicious cycle: People enter it with few skills, and no one wants to pay good wages for workers with few skills. Because the pay is low, the likelihood is that those with little training and few skills will take up the work. How can we break this cycle? While we must acknowledge that there are poor teachers at work, even among those with extensive training, good in-service education can help. But what may be required for a real break in the cycle is public understanding and recognition of the potential benefits of high-quality education in the early years and deeper public commitment to the welfare of young children.

It is not uncommon for laypersons to point out that they know of an outstanding teacher who has had no training. Perhaps all of us have encountered just such a gifted or "natural" teacher. This claim is, however, a dangerous one. Abraham Lincoln was a self-taught lawyer, but virtually everything about him was exceptional. Furthermore, there was a great deal less to be learned by lawyers in his time. The main point here is that a profession can never be designed on the basis of its exceptions. On the contrary, professional training is designed to provide *all* its practitioners with minimal standards to help them perform effectively. If all lawyers had Lincoln's remarkable qualities of mind and could teach themselves as thoroughly as he did, we might have no need for law schools.

Specialized Knowledge

Scholars seem to agree that a major defining attribute of a profession is that it is an occupation whose practices are based on specialized knowledge. This knowledge is thought to have several characteristics:

1. The knowledge is abstract rather than concrete (as in the case of crafts, sports, trades, or bureaucracies).
2. The knowledge consists of principles that are reasonably reliable generalizations to be considered in the course of practicing the profession. Some scholars insist that the knowledge underlying professional practice is organized into a systematic body of principles.
3. The knowledge and principles are relevant to practical rather than metaphysical or academic concerns. They are intended to rationalize the techniques of the profession and, as such, are oriented to some kind of practical and socially useful end.
4. The body of knowledge is esoteric or exclusive in that it is known only to practitioners of the profession and is unknown to laypeople. In this sense, the profession has a monopoly on most of its relevant knowledge and techniques.
5. Practitioners belong to professional societies that take responsibility for disseminating new knowledge relevant to practice by producing scholarly journals and by providing conferences and workshops through which members are kept informed.

Can we identify the body of knowledge, specify the reliable principles, and develop a consensus as to the best available practices that will serve as a basis for professional practice in early childhood education? It is not clear what procedures are to be followed in finding answers to these questions. We each might begin by listing those principles we consider essential and worthy of inclusion and then examining the list in a systematic way. To what extent would we agree on our lists? Finding answers to these questions is one of the biggest tasks ahead of us.

Some principles I wish to nominate for inclusion in our professioal body of specialized knowledge are outlined very briefly below. These assertions are derived from my own understanding of what constitutes the best practice and my interpretation of the literature on children's learning and development.

1. Teaching strategies and curriculum decisions are best when they take into account both the value of immediate experiences and their long-term benefits. Teaching and curriculum practices that keep children busy and/or amused in the short term may or may not provide a solid foundation for the long course of learning and development.
2. Young children's learning is optimized by engaging them in interaction and in active rather than passive activities.
3. Many of the experiences or factors that influence development and learning are likely to be most beneficial when they occur in optimal rather than extreme amounts, intensities, or frequencies. In terms of

teaching strategies, for example, the help, attention, or stimulation given can be both too little or too great for the development of a given individual's self-reliance. Likewise, the extent to which the curriculum includes routines can also be excessive or insufficient for the management of the life of a group of children.

4. The curriculum for young children is oriented toward helping them to make better sense of their own environment and experiences. As children grow, the concepts, ideas, and topics introduced are extended to include environments and experiences of others.

5. Many aspects of development and learning have the characteristic of a recursive cycle in that once a child has a behavior pattern, the chances are that others will respond to him or her in such a way that the pattern will be strengthened. Thus, for example, a child who is unlikable is very likely to be responded to with rejection and to respond to rejection in such a way as to become more unlikable. A related principle of development is that a child cannot effect a change on his or her own; the adult must intervene to interrupt the recursive cycle.

6. The more informal the learning environment, the more access the teacher has to information about where the child is in terms of development and learning. The more informed the teacher is, the more likely he or she is to be able to make appropriate decisions about what teaching strategies to use and what curriculum activities to introduce. A related principle is that the life of the group is likely to be enhanced by optimum rather than maximum informality.

7. The three basic functions of language—communication, expression, and reason—are acquired and strengthened through conversation rather than by passive exposure or systematic instruction.

8. Young children's development and learning are enhanced by a curriculum including activities and materials that provide them with content for conversation that is relevant, vivid, interesting, familiar, and/or significant to them.

9. Appropriate teaching strategies and curricula are those that take into account the acquisition of knowledge, skills, *and* dispositions, especially the dispositions to go on learning and to apply the knowledge and skills acquired. Emphasis on the acquisition of knowledge and on practicing skills is excessive when it undermines such dispositions as curiosity, creativity, and other types of intrinsic motivation.

10. The younger children are, the greater variety of teaching strategies and the greater the flexibility of the curriculum required. The use of a single pedagogical method or narrow range of curriculum materials and activities increases the likelihood that a significant proportion of children will experience feelings of incompetence.

Many more principles can be added to these 10, and I urge members of the early childhood community both as individuals and as members of a professional society to develop and share more.

WHAT LIES AHEAD?

It seems to me that the research on development and learning currently being reported in the journals is much more applicable to pedagogical practice than it was when I first entered the field 20 years ago. In Britain, the work of such scholars as Clark (Clark & Wade, 1983), Wells (1983), Donaldson (1983), Dunn (Dunn & Dale, 1984), Karmiloff–Smith (1984), Rutter (Garmezy & Rutter, 1983) and many others is rich in implications for principles of education in the early years. In the United States, the list of scholars whose work supports the "informal," or intellectually rather than academically oriented, approach to early childhood education is also long. I commend the research of Brown (Brown & Campione, 1984), Nelson (Nelson & Seidman, 1984), Gottman (1983), Carpenter (1983), and Rogoff (1982), among many others. These investigators support the view that — with the help of very skilled, observant, attentive, reflective, and thoughtful adults — children construct their own understandings and sharpen their skills through interaction with their environment. In this sense, it seems to me that contemporary developmental researchers are painstakingly rediscovering the insights of John Dewey.

I recently came across a copy of D. E. M. Gardner's *Testing results in the infant school,* a book published in England in 1941 and not widely known among early childhood educators in the United States. I was surprised to find that Gardner begins by describing two contrasting types of infant schools. Although she refers to the two types as School A and School B, we would most likely refer to one as formal and academic and the other as informal or child-centered. These descriptions can be used almost verbatim to characterize contrasting early childhood education settings today in many parts of the world. The basic arguments Gardner makes about appropriate learning environments for young children still have to be made today. Although current research on children's intellectual development reaffirms Gardner's views on how children learn, we have yet to marshal the kind of compelling evidence we need to prove that the methods advocated by Gardner (1941) and Marianne Parry (1986) are more effective than others — particularly in the long term.

There are several reasons why we cannot produce the kind of persuasive empirical evidence we need. First, it is difficult to conduct longitudinal studies of young children and their teachers that would take into account the accepted canons of social science research. It seems as though the more rigorous the research design, the less relevant or valid the data, and vice versa. Second, to conduct investigations that would satisfy standard scientific requirements would very likely be unethical: It it unethical to subject others to experiences one has reason to suspect may not be good for them for the sake of research—or for any other purpose.

Inevitably, then, we work in a field in which reliable data are difficult to obtain. In any field in which the data base is slippery, the informational vacuum is filled by ideologies or doctrines (i.e., systems of beliefs that we hold most strongly about the things of which we are least certain). Thus, our commitment to particular approaches, even in the absence of compelling evidence that they are best or right, is in the nature of the field. However, the risks attendant upon such conditions are that we tend to reject counterevidence and resist others' views. A professional code of ethics should remind us to keep an open mind, to look carefully at all the available evidence, to identify clearly our stands as being based respectively on evidence, on experience, and on ideology. Such reminders are among the important functions of professional societies. It may be that, when we are clear about the bases of our views, we shall be better able to increase public understanding of them and thereby gain their support in our efforts to improve provisions for young children.

REFERENCES

Becker, H.S. (1962). The nature of a profession. In N.B. Henry (Ed.), *Education for the professions* (pp. 27–46). National Society for the Study of Education Yearbook. Chicago: National Society for the Study of Education.

Broudy, H.S. (1983). The humanities and their uses: Proper claims and expectations. *Journal of Aesthetic Education, 17*(4), 125–148.

Brown, A.L., & Campione, J.C. (1984). Three faces of transfer: Implications for early competence, individual differences, and instruction. In M.E. Lamb, A. L. Brown, & B. Rogof (Eds.), *Advances in developmental psychology* (Vol. 3, pp. 143–192). Hillsdale, NJ: Erlbaum.

Brown, C.C., & Gottfried, A. (1985). *Play interactions: The role of toys and parental involvement in children's development.* Pediatric Round Table 11. Skillman, NJ: Johnson & Johnson.

Carpenter, J. (1983). Activity structure and play: Implications for socialization. In M.B. Liss. (Ed.), *Social and cognitive skills: Sex roles and children's play* (pp. 117–143). New York: Academic.

Clark, M.M., & Wade, B. (1983). Early childhood education [Special issue]. *Educational Review, 5,*(2).

Consortium for Longitudinal Studies. (1983). *As the twig is bent.* Hillsdale, NJ: Erlbaum.

Cummings, E.M., Iannotti, R.J., & Zahn-Waxler, C. (1985). Influence of conflict between adults on the emotions and aggression of young children. *Developmental Psychology, 21*(3), 495–507.

Donaldson, M. (1983). Children's reasoning. In M. Donaldson, R. Grieve, & C. Pratt (Eds.), *Early childhood development and education* (pp. 231–236). London: Guilford.

Dunn, J., & Dale, N. (1984). Collaboration in joint pretend. In I. Bretherton (Ed.), *Symbolic play: The development of social understanding* (pp. 131–157). New York: Academic.

Forsyth, P.B., & Danisiewicz, T.J. (1983). Toward a theory of professionalization. In P. Silver (Ed.), *Professionalism in educational administration* (pp. 39–45). Victoria, Australia: Deakin University Press.

Gardner, D.E.M. (1941). *Testing results in the infant school.* London: Methuen.

Garmezy, N., & Rutter, M. (Eds.) (1983). *Stress, coping and development in children.* New York: McGraw-Hill.

Goode, W.J. (1983). The theoretical limits of professionalization. In P. Silver (Ed.), *Professionalism in educational administration* (pp. 46–67). Victoria, Australia: Deakin University Press.

Gottman, J.M. (1983). How children become friends. *Monographs of the Society for Research in Child Development, 48,*(3, Serial No. 201).

Green, T.F. (1983). Excellence, equity, and equality. In L. Shulman & G. Sykes (Eds.), *Handbook of teaching and policy (pp. 318–341).* New York: Longmans.

Haskins, R. (1985). Public school aggression in children with varying day-care experiences. *Child Development, 56,* 689–703.

Karmiloff–Smith, A. (1984). Children's problem solving. In M. Lamb, A. Brown, & B. Rogoff (Eds.), *Advances in developmental psychology* (Vol. 3, pp. 39–90). Hillsdale, NJ: Erlbaum.

Katz, L.G. (1977). *Talks with teachers.* Washington, DC: National Association for the Education of Young Children.

Katz, L.G. (1984a). Contemporary perspectives on the roles of mothers and teachers. In L.G. Katz, *More talks with teachers* (pp. 1–26). Urbana, IL: ERIC Clearinghouse on Elementary and Early Childhood Education.

Katz, L.G. (1984b). The education of preprimary teachers. In L.G. Katz, P.J. Wagemaker, & K. Steiner (Eds.), *Current topics in early childhood education* (Vol. 5, pp. 209–227). Norwood, NJ: Ablex.

Katz, L.G. (1984c). Ethical issues in working with young children. In L.G. Katz, *More talks with teachers* (pp. 45–60). Urbana, IL: ERIC Clearinghouse on Elementary and Early Childhood Education.

Katz, L.G. & Becher, R.M. (1985, November). *Professionalism in teacher–parent relations.* Paper presented at the annual conference of the National Association for the Education of Young Children, New Orleans.

Katz, L.G., & Raths, J.D. (1986). A framework for research on teacher education programs. *Journal of Teacher Education, 26,*(6), 9–15.

Nelson, K., & Seidman, S. (1984). Playing with scripts. In I. Bretherton (Ed.), *Symbolic play: The development of social understanding* (pp. 45–71). New York: Academic.

Parry, E.M. (1986). Working with young children is a bold adventure. In P. Heaslip (Ed.), *The challenge of the future: Professional Issues in Early Childhood Education.* Bristol, England: Bristol Polytechnics.

Rogoff, B. (1982). Integrating context and cognitive development. In M.E. Lamb & A.L. Brown (Eds.), *Advances in developmental psychology* (Vol. 2, pp. 125–170). Hillsdale, NJ: Erlbaum.

Schlechty, P.C., & Vance, V.S. (1981). Do academically able teachers leave education? The North Carolina case. *Phi Delta Kappan, 63*(2), 106–112.

Silin, J. (1985). Authority as knowledge: A problem of professionalization. *Young Children,* March, 41–46.

Wells, G. (1983). Talking with children: The complementary roles of parents and teachers. In M. Donaldson, R. Grieve, & C. Pratt (Eds.), *Early childhood development and education* (pp. 127–150). London: Guilford.

Wolfle, L. M. (1978). *Prestige in an American university.* Paper presented at the annual meeting of the American Educational Research Association, Toronto, Canada.

AUTHOR NOTE

This chapter is based on a paper presented at the Early Childhood Organisation Conference in honor of Miss E. Marianne Parry, O.B.E., Bristol Polytechnic, Bristol, England, September 20, 1985.

2

The Early Childhood Educator's Knowledge Base: A Reconsideration

Jonathan G. Silin

Long Island Association for AIDS Care

Within the broad domains of educational praxis, people committed to early childhood education have always displayed a unique sense of mission. Recently, Bernard Spodek (1984) invited early childhood educators to renew this sense of mission, this common identity, by examining the history of this field and the issues that have consistently informed its discourse. This chapter was written in response to Spodek's invitation and explores one aspect of this past, the knowledge base upon which early educators have relied for making curricular decisions. Such an exploration is particularly interesting, for, despite the distinct sense of mission possessed by most in the field—perhaps even because of a certain forgetfulness about the history that has shaped the profession—early educators have borrowed heavily from some academic disciplines while totally ignoring others in order to rationalize existing practices and to project new ones.

In the 20th century, the field of early childhood education has been most permeable to the influence of psychologists, and psychology has become its primary "supply" discipline. Thus, theoretical discussions about curricular goals have been predicated upon distinctions within psychological rather than educational paradigms (Kohlberg & Mayer, 1972). Training programs for new teachers have been designed to reflect different approaches to development (Seaver & Cartwright, 1977), teacher training has been analyzed in terms of the psychological theory employed by the practitioner (Porter, 1981), and programmatic innovations have been evaluated in terms of developmental appropriateness (Elkind, 1981). This "psychologistic" orientation became most pronounced in the 1960s with the proliferation of Head Start models. Whether one was a behaviorist advocating a narrowly academic agenda, a Piagetian offering a somewhat broader conception of intellectual growth, or a developmental-interactionist focusing on socioemotional issues, psychological criteria became the basis for educational decision making.

Today, despite some changes in the field, the discourse of early childhood education continues to give precedence to psychological considerations, acknowledging in only a cursory way that other concerns may be of importance (Weber, 1984). But these other concerns, referred to as philosophical or value-related, rarely as economically or politically relevant, seldom receive full treatment in the literature. For example, Evans (1982), in his description of the components of early childhood programs, states that these programs' theoretical foundations rest equally in philosophical and psychological thought. But when he refers to the terms currently used to identify different models, he unwittingly reveals the dominance of the latter over the former:

> Over time, however, certain bodies of consistent, integrated thought about philosophy and psychology have come to dominate curriculum models for early childhood education. The bodies of thought are identified by various labels, such as the *behaviorist, dynamic* and *constructivist* approaches. . . . (p. 110)

It is the purpose of this chapter to examine how and why this reliance on a psychological perspective has come about, as well as to suggest what might be considered problematic in the current state of affairs: the way that the psychological lens focuses our regard in some directions and not in others, the implicit value structures of developmental perspectives, and the implications of misconstruing psychological goals and categories for educational ones. In a more general way, this chapter examines how the special sense of mission and the identity that undergirds the profession have functioned for early educators in the past and questions how the field might best be served in the future.

HISTORICAL PERSPECTIVE

Understanding the present begins with interpreting the past. The beginnings of early education might be traced to the 16th century and the recognition that young children are not simply immature adults or to the publication of important pedagogical treatises by Comenius, Locke, and Rousseau acknowledging the importance of the early years. However, it was Froebel's work that most surely catalyzed that early education movement in America. A man of deep religious convictions, Froebel claimed to base his program on a series of revealed truths—the unity of life, whole/part relations, the interconnection of all things, and the law of opposites. He designed a series of pedagogical apparatuses and exercises, the gifts and the occupations, to symbolize these truths and to make them evident to children. As a rationalist, Froebel was less concerned with teaching specific content than with helping children to recognize universal values. He conceived of education as a process of "unfoldment" through which children were given the opportunity to make the inner outer and the outer inner.

A challenge to the Froebelian kindergarten ultimately was mounted during the last decade of the 19th century by those for whom scientific method and direct observation took precedence over religious conviction and intuited forms of knowledge. Based in a philosophy of pragmatism rather than idealism, the progressives believed that the early childhood curriculum should be built on psychological rather than logical principles. They were convinced that real experiences expressing the immediate interests of children, rather than symbolic materials revealing eternal verities, should form the core of curriculum and that the teacher should act as democratic guide rather than as authoritarian director of activities. According to the reformers, schools should help children learn appropriate behavior through social interaction and the reconstruction of experience rather than through the imitation of moral models. Thus, the progressive educators wanted not only to change the very look and feel of the early childhood classroom but also to modify the knowledge base on which it was constructed.

The shift from a religious/philosophical knowledge base to a secular/psychological one was consistent with the 19th-century demand for scientific legitimation in all fields of endeavor. It might also be said to have been imminent in the 1859 publication of Darwin's *The origin of species* just 3 years after the opening of the first German-language kindergarten in America. Although it was Darwin's use of the scientific method that shaped the mind-set of the century, it was the popularity of evolutionary theory itself that created new interest in the mental life of children. The concept of change over time as a progressive evolution from primitive to sophisticated structural forms was extended from biology, to anthropology, to child study. Borrowing from the embryologists, educators asserted that, just as individual members of a species repeat the stages of evolution experienced by their phyla in prenatal development, so humans after birth recapitulate the stages of cultural change undergone by humankind as a whole. This assertion made for an inevitable equation of the primitive with the childlike that had political implications for non-European people and pedagogical ramifications for children (Gould, 1981). Thus, to be meaningful and efficient, education had to be child-centered, or based on the developmentally determined interests of the child.

In the United States, it was G. Stanley Hall's child study movement, with its emphasis on the direct observation of children and questionnaire inquiries rather than intuited insights or introspective recall of childhood memories, that provided the knowledge of children upon which appropriate educational environments were to be structured. Although signaling the acceptance of what later was to be called the child development point of view, child study itself soon lost ground to the new science of child development. Child development psychologists wanted to create a more rigorous approach to data collection by employing objective, quantitative measures; standardized testing techniques; and experimental laboratory procedures. They sought acceptance by the more traditional sciences through the use of such positivist methodologies and through disassociating themselves from the more practical concerns of educators and parents. The professionalization of child study clearly involved a growing distinction between those who produced knowledge about children and those who were to use such knowledge (Takanishi, 1981). This expert/implementer dichotomy and the hierarchy of functions that goes along with it appears to be an inescapable outcome of positivist science and the technical-mindedness that pervades education today (Fay, 1975).

In the 20th century, the field of early education has reflected a particular permeability to the knowledge created by psychologists. The 1920s, for example, saw the dominance of behaviorist theories of learning and the measurement movement, as well as concern for the formation of proper habits. Although this influence remained strong in the kindergarten, perhaps because it seemed well suited to programs designed to prepare children for the elementary grades, during the 1930s other early childhood institutions, such as the nursery school, were more affected by the dissemination of Freudian theory. Then, in the 1940s and 1950s, the role of normative studies of children like those done by Gesell at Yale firmly took hold. The widespread use of normative studies marks the success of the well-articulated child development point of view. As defined by Jersild (1946), this meant

> an effort to apply to the education of children lessons learned from the study of children themselves. Research in child development has provided many findings which have implications for education. . . . But the child development approach does not represent merely a collection of facts. It represents a point of view.
>
> Basic to this point of view is a spirit of inquiry — a desire to learn about the ways of children . . . with this spirit of inquiry goes an attitude of respect for children at all stages of their growth. (p. 182)

Today, it is the literature of psychological development that remains the primary base from which educational decisions about young children in school are made. That is, despite the pervasive shift in the 1960s and 1970s to more cognitively oriented curricula and the somewhat less prominent role given to socioemotional adjustment, early educators continue to rely almost exclusively on psychological rationales for program design. The substitution of Piaget for Gesell and Berlyne for Freud, may change the specifics of the early childhood knowledge base, but it does not alter the terrain in which it is located. As Bettye Caldwell (1984), past president of the National Association for the Education of Young Children, confidently summarized, "Our field represents the applied side of the basic science of child development" (p. 53).

EDUCATIONAL INTERESTS AND PSYCHOLOGICAL THEORY

For some, the role of psychology in education has been seen as more problematic. For example, Spodek (1970) makes an important distinction between curriculum sources and resources, noting that, while the former are "a set of goals which are the aims of education" (p. 6), the latter are only a means to help achieve these ends. Among the resources are certainly developmental theory and learning theory. Egan (1983), in a more extensive analysis, has asserted that the specific function of educational theory, as opposed to psychological theory, is to tell us how to design curricula to produce educated people. A deceptively simple definition, at its core is a concern for the kind of person who will result from the educational process. To project the nature of the end product of education — the educated person — is to project the kind of context in which this person can reach his or her full potential. A theory of education is not only a theory of individual growth but also a theory of political and social power. If the goal of education is to inculcate the knowledge and skills that will prepare persons to be successful political and social agents, then it must be informed by a sense of the *polis* that the student will eventually enter.

In Egan's view, psychological theory is not only different from but secondary to educational theory. The former becomes meaningful only as it is part of the latter. In fact, the role of education is to shape the forces that produce psychological regularities, not to be bound by them. This situation is the case because psychological research is concerned with behaviors and thoughts that are the result of personal and historical experience. Psychology reflects what has been and what is, but not necessarily what ought to be. Psychologists, whose goal is the pursuit of knowledge, can afford to isolate particular skills or characteristics for study and can at least claim to be objective in their practices. The work of educators, on the other hand, is more clearly culture-bound and value-saturated because it prepares children to live within specific communities and traditions. Thus, it must not be concerned only with cognitive and socioemotional skills but also with erudition.

Educated people need to be able to think clearly and make wise choices as to what they will think about. But many still believe that knowledge about early education settings should be created by psychologists rather than by educators themselves. This belief undoubtedly has contributed to the tension that exists between practitioner and researcher (Katz, 1977). Because educators are the lower status group, supposedly concerned with practice rather than theory, it has been too easily assumed that their interests might be subsumed under the interests of the more prestigious group. However, those who choose to see early childhood education as a unique cultural system with its own history, tradition, and values suggest otherwise (Takanishi, 1981). They point out that, because early educators go through a specific socialization process, they see children and development differently from child development specialists. And because they work in classrooms, rather than laboratories, they have a different perspective on what is essential in order to understand early education settings and even possess alternative conceptions of education itself.

The Piagetian Paradigm

Perhaps the limitations of the psychological perspective for the educator can best be understood through a brief analysis of Piaget's work (Piaget, 1954). Becoming popular at a time of mounting concern over math/science education and growing interest in the open classroom, Piaget's theories are now a pervasive influence in early childhood education. More than psychodynamic theory, with its limited implications for curriculum design, or behavior modification strategies, which have been confined to specific program models, Piagetian constructs have directly affected a wide variety of early childhood programs. And although Piaget's theory is clearly exceptional in its richness and complexity, its very popularity speaks as much to its uniqueness as to its representation of widely accepted assumptions about development. Criticisms of Piaget's work also underline the difficulty of producing objective, definitive research about subjects who are by nature immature, unstable, and not given to the controls of experimental procedures.

Decontextualized knowledge. In the 1920s, when Piaget's work first was translated into English, mainstream American psychology was dominated by behaviorism and procedures relying on quantitative data for validation. Piaget's structuralist hypotheses and clinical method were inimical to these principles. His writings did not find a very large audience.

Ironically, it was an English educator, Susan Isaacs (1966), working not from a behaviorist position but from a psychoanalytical one, who offered the most trenchant commentary of Piaget's method. Her concerns were not that Piaget's findings lacked the corroboration of large-scale studies, but rather that the clinical interview itself did not promote the optimal use of the child's intelligence. Isaacs believed that many of the interview questions tested the possession of specific pieces of information rather than the ability to reason, as Piaget claimed. In the interview, questions were asked *of* children, not *by* them, and were thus suggestive of particular answers and related to limited, stereotyped situations. Children's intelligent thought was not revealed because children were neither naturally interested nor motivated to seek answers to questions raised by others. Alternatively, Isaacs suggested that reason was best studied in real-life situations where it arose spontaneously in response to the child's desire to find out about the world and to solve meaningful problems.

In a more recent work, Donaldson (1978) reviews a series of experiments that replicated, with slight but important modifications, those done by Piaget on decentering, class inclusion, deductive thought, and conservation (Piaget, 1954). She concludes that children's success in these experiments was influenced by their knowledge of language, their assessment of what the experimenter intended, and the manner in which they would represent the situation to themselves whether or not the experimenter was actually present. Performance level was affected by minor changes in language, format, apparatus, and procedure. Failure to deal successfully with many tasks, according to Donaldson, reflects the adult's inability to decenter, to understand the world from the child's viewpoint, and not necessarily the child's inability to use reason. Donaldson's findings, consistent with Isaacs's earlier assertions, suggest that Piaget's conclusions are ill founded because children fail to grasp the nature of the problem being presented to them, or the problem is irrelevant and they lack appropriate motivation to seek an adequate answer to it. Although Isaacs and Donaldson have similar criticisms of Piaget, these lead Isaacs to insist on the role of the school as supporting the child's learning in the context of his or her ongoing experiences. They suggest to Donaldson that the school must articulate and provide more direct instruction in the abstract, disembedded forms of thought valued by Piaget and society at large.

Egan (1983), in a more broadly based analysis of Piaget's work, deals with some of the conceptual questions implied but left unexplored by Donaldson. He raises doubts as to whether Piaget described a natural, universal pattern of development, as claimed, or whether he described only that which was the result of particular methods of sociocultural initiation. Egan marshals cross-cultural evidence to suggest that Piaget's stages are not universal or invariant in sequence; this evidence casts doubt on Piaget's explanations of why children at certain stages can perform some tasks but not others—specifically on the ambiguous role attributed to experience and the meaning of *décalage*. If, as Egan maintains, Piaget's stages reflect a logical rather than a psychological necessity, then they are not amenable to proofs from empirical data at all, and their scientific validity is again thrown into question. Further, Egan's analysis leads him to skepticism about educational commonplaces drawn from Piaget's theory, such as the active nature of learning, the importance of readiness, and the assessment of individual differences.

Reason and values in psychology.   As a group, the authors discussed so far are representative of those who have questioned Piaget's method, his resultant data base, and the nature of his theory qua theory. In a more general way, they provoke us to examine how psychological research is conducted and to question whether its methods are consistent with the more contextualized, less fragmented ways early educators experience growing children. There are others, however, who are less concerned with method-ological issues than with the emphasis given to logico-mathematical struc-tures in Piaget's work. These commentators help us to recognize the fact that competing schools within developmental psychology focus on different aspects of human potential and contain alternative world views.

It is not surprising, therefore, that Piaget's theory, with its concern for the development of rational modes of thought, has arisen in a world dominated by technological accomplishments and scientific approaches to the manage-ment of human problems. What Piaget's theory excludes from consideration are nonrational, but not necessarily irrational, modes of thought: intuitive, mythical, religious. This omission is not a neutral exclusion; a definite value system is operative in the Piagetian framework. Take, for example, Piaget's understanding of symbolic play (Piaget, 1962). For him, play is a function of underdeveloped thinking processes. Play is significant when young children's needs to assimilate information, to distort reality to conform to their existing picture of the world, is greatest. As their cognitive structures become more adequate, as they accommodate more to reality, children enter the period of concrete operations, when they lose their need to engage in symbolic play and become interested in rule-governed games. To Piaget, imaginative play is a compensatory activity rather than a source of new concepts or ideas and is clearly irrelevant to adult functioning.

Piaget is concerned with directed rather than with creative, imaginative, or divergent forms of thought. Play is therefore interpreted as an epiphen-omenon, with no inherent value, though admittedly it may serve a cathartic purpose in the emotional lives of the young. In contrast to this view, others (Herron & Sutton–Smith, 1971) see play as a primary phenomenon, as an essential mode of being in childhood, with its own structures, purposes, and sources for generating novel ideas. If play is considered an end in itself, it may represent an irreducible challenge to contemporary values. That is, because play is a nonproductive, pleasure-oriented, aesthetic activity, it may be seen to threaten a society built on material production, repression, and control. To some (Alves, 1972), play expresses the child's refusal to be organized by adult conceptions of reality.

To accept the Piagetian epistemology as the basis for educational pro-gramming is to accept a particular conception of what is essential to human development and to success in adult life. This conception is most consistent with a highly rationalized, scientifically oriented culture. To accept Piaget is to accept his belief that intelligent action is the human expression of the biological process of adaptation (Piaget, 1950). The implication is that education, in promoting intelligent behavior, promotes adaptation to the environment. In the end, every psychology is embedded not only in a world view but also in a politic, and the politics of adaptation are certainly not the politics of resistance or revolution.

Those, like Merleau–Ponty (1964), who are critical of the key role given to logico-mathematical reasoning in Piagetian theory raise issues that have general implications for the use of any theory of development in the determination of educational contexts. First, they point to the way that psychological theories define our perspectives, shape our interpretations of common childhood activities, and contain specific value judgments. Second, they call to our attention the fact that psychological theories exist within the framework of the positivist sciences. As a knowledge base, the exclusive use of such theories devalues alternative ways of knowing children — aesthetic, symbolic, imaginative. Whereas educational decisions are based, or should be based, on more than our knowledge of children, it is how and what we choose to know about children that is immediately in question.

The developmental metaphor. Finally, a third group of Piaget's critics can be connected by their common concern for the way that his stage theory of development functions to assure an absolute distinction between childhood and adulthood. Merleau–Ponty (1964), for example, suggests that the Piagetian conception of cognitive structures sacrifices the immediate, visceral knowledge of self and others that we possess before being overwhelmed by language and rules of perception. He believes that Piaget's hierarchy of stages posits an artificial separation of children from adults. Merleau–Ponty prefers to look for continuities, the child as neither absolute other nor as exactly the same as ourselves. Such continuity comes from assuming the centrality of preconceptual knowledge, knowledge that is neither objective nor subjective but that emerges through direct participation in the world. This is knowledge that allows us to know both the child in the classroom and the child within ourselves.

In recent years, growing numbers of early childhood educators have come to view stage theories of development more metaphorically than literally (Weber, 1984). While this trend probably closely reflects scientific thinking, it throws into question their usefulness to curriculum design and meaning for the educator.

If Piaget's perspective is one that ultimately sees children as incomplete beings, falling short of adult standards of functioning, part of the explanation lies in his belief in the superiority of reason over other forms of knowing. But part of the explanation also resides in the basic metaphor of development itself. This is a metaphor borrowed from the biological sciences; its use implies not only a continuity of physical and psychological growth but also an adult-centered perspective in relation to children. Research making this assumption begins with a set of adult characteristics, usually defined by middle-class Western standards of maturity, and examines growth as progress toward the achievement of these characteristics (Speier, 1976). The imposition of these standards is rationalized through the further assumption that, because developmental processes are biologically based and best exemplified in Piaget's assimilation/accommodation model of adaptation, they are also universal. Although environment or experience may affect the speed of development, the attainment of higher levels of thought, or even the way that specific tasks are accomplished, the sequence of stages and the laws of development are assumed to be cross-culturally valid.

PERENNIAL PROBLEMS IN EARLY CHILDHOOD EDUCATION

When educators rely on psychologists such as Piaget for their knowledge base, they may be avoiding difficult philosophical and social issues while believing themselves to be acting in a "professional" manner. They also may be succumbing to a subtle, but nonetheless potent, form of technical-mindedness because they are taking educational decision making out of the realm of moral and political consideration where it more properly belongs. Early educators are particularly vulnerable to this form of instrumental rationality because they tend to regard themselves as objective, if well-intentioned, protectors of the young and because they are members of a low-status field seeking to improve its position in a society that places primacy on scientific knowledge (Silin, 1982). Age-related differences should not be obscured in developing educational environments; nonetheless, what age means needs to be explored from many perspectives, and knowledge about how people change over time should be part of an articulated social philosophy.

The absence of such a social theory component in early childhood programs underlines the limits of the current knowledge base and contributes to two perennial problems. The first is the ongoing issue of curriculum content for young children. The nature of appropriate knowledge for the young, often ill defined, has been a source of controversy among early educators (Evans, 1982). Diverse conceptions of the child's developmental abilities, concerns, and needs have led to differing approaches to curriculum design (Maccoby & Zellner, 1970). But perhaps it is the overriding preoccupation with developmental correctness itself that has left early educators without clear guidelines for content selection. If education is about initiating the young into an already existing world, if it is to teach them not only how to live but also what the world is really like, then psychological process considerations are probably insufficient to the task.

The second problem is very much intertwined with the first since it involves the basis for the educator's professional expertise. Is such expertise grounded in the educator's knowledge of child development, understanding of materials, ability to teach correct school behaviors, or nurturing personality? Beside these usual conceptions, given the nature of educational theory proposed here, professional knowledge might also be grounded in a sociopolitical analysis of society or an ethical vision of the world in which the child will one day participate. But the reliance on psychological research for validating program decisions and the resultant ambiguity about content and traditional conceptualizations of the teacher's role (Almy, 1975) mediate against such considerations in early childhood thinking. The reaction, or lack thereof, to the growing body of literature looking at education from a critical social theory perspective exemplifies this attempt to keep the field clear of any debates in which its self-declared mandate to protect the young might be questioned. The limited response of early childhood educators to political critiques of education also may be explained in terms of weaknesses in the analyses themselves (i.e., their failure to address early education) the self-image of early childhood educators, and gender-related social expectations of female professionals (Silin, 1985).

Although sensitive to public demands for greater emphasis on the academic potential of young children, early educators have tended to ignore or to deem irrelevant the criticisms coming from educational historians and sociologists in the late 1960s. This was the period when revisionist historians (Katz, 1971; Tyack, 1974) described the failure of the schools to promote social mobility, equality of opportunity, and democratic forms of interaction—and when radical critics of the schools (Illich, 1970; Kohl, 1967) focused on issues of depersonalization, apathy, and alienation within educational institutions. It was also a time when educationists (Giroux, 1980; Macdonald, 1975) concerned themselves with the nature of the curriculum, overt and covert, and the way it was being structured to fulfill the socioeconomic needs of the postindustrial world.

It is true that, for a brief period during the War on Poverty, early educators tried to address the issue of the relationships among social class, curriculum, and schooling outcomes. This interest took the form of a debate over the nature of compensatory education. While some (Bereiter & Engelmann, 1966) argued that children of the poor needed more academically oriented programs in order to catch up to their middle-class peers, others (Biber, Shapiro, & Wickens, 1971) maintained that all children, regardless of background, benefited from the same kind of developmentally oriented approach. From the beginning of this debate, a few (Lazerson, 1971) were skeptical of the ability of educators to effect changes that were more properly required in the economic system outside the classroom. The majority of educators, however, seemed to have been caught up in the belief that education could in fact equalize opportunity and create a more just society. This early enthusiasm has quickly tempered, and interest in compensatory education has since been subsumed under discussions of the value of bilingual and multicultural programs, thus masking economic issues. Even within minority groups, disagreement exists about whether schools should stress unique cultural histories and personal meanings or public knowledge and academic skills (Rodriguez, 1982). Although the former may better enable children to tell their own stories and to be at home in the culture of their birth, the latter may better prepare them to survive in the larger society.

The beginnings of the Head Start and Follow Through programs can be attributed less to a recognition of systematic weaknesses in the schools than to the limited acknowledgment that problems existed in the society at large for which education could compensate. To early educators, the need for revised curricula was not so much an indictment of what existed as a return to an older theme of the field—the amelioration of social ills through education. Indeed, a concern for bettering the circumstances of the poor was one of the distinguishing characteristics of those who first created early childhood programs; this theme connects the work of such diverse individuals as Rachel and Margaret Macmillan, Maria Montessori, Robert Owen, and Johann Pestalozzi. The new research on the importance of the early years for later cognitive development (Bloom, 1964; Hunt, 1961) could easily be used as a rationale for revising programs. A more political indictment of the system qua system might thus be avoided: The revisionist critique need not apply.

Future Directions

Early childhood education is a unique field of study and action whose practitioners often possess a strong sense of mission. At the level of the individual teacher, teacher-educator, or researcher, this sense of mission usually is expressed in the belief that young children require special forms of nurturance and care. But as members of a collective enterprise, it is important for early childhood educators to recognize the degree to which such an identity is embedded in the history of a field with its own socializing institutions, sites of practice, and tools of instruction. It also is important to recognize the nature of the knowledge base that has been used to guide both theory and practice. It seems clear that, if early childhood educators are to attain the professional recognition they deserve and if they are to maintain their distinct identity within the larger educational sphere, they must strengthen the knowledge base from which they work.

To broaden the early childhood knowledge base is to accept that schooling, even nursery schooling, is one of the central ways that our society organizes power and influence. It is also to acknowledge that early education should not be exempt from a more political analysis of its programs than has hitherto taken place. From this perspective, teaching needs to be viewed as more than the professionalization of a maternal function occurring in a protective, hermetically sealed vacuum. Rather, teaching must be seen in the context of larger societal processes that both shape and are shaped by it. In one of the few attempts to assess the economic implications of the expansion of early education, Chamboredon and Prevort (1975) stress the need for such a change in our thinking:

> The conditions for understanding nursery-school exercises flow from the conditions for inventing these exercises. . . . The proper objective of a sociology of nursery-school practice is the analysis of the lag between the functions delegated to the school by different social classes and the functions which it objectively tends to fulfill. (p. 334)

Drawing on sources from sociology, philosophy, and history, as well as from psychology, early childhood educators might then move away from their traditional developmental, "individual needs" language, which frequently masks the real impact of their work. An undue emphasis on individual development and change can lead to a neglect of the need for transformation of the social and economic realities of everyday life and to a denial of the teacher's potential as a political actor. Even the smallest pedagogical acts may have meanings for students that extend beyond the classroom. If teachers are to be more fully in control of their professional lives, they must assess these meanings and incorporate them into their knowledge base.

Using universal, theoretical constructs also can obfuscate the complex realities of children's lives. Literature and the arts may therefore provide much-needed access to direct ways of knowing and understanding children. Such investigations undoubtedly will lead to a renewed respect for the common ground between children and adults so frequently hidden in hierarchically organized stage theories of development. A few theorists within the field of early education already have begun to move in such a direction by emphasizing the uniqueness and integrity of each child. In this phenomenological approach, "the existential moment-by-moment environmental interaction of the learner supersedes an interest in — even a recognition of — developmental factors. The departure from stage theory is due in part to discomfiture with a designated end point for all children" (Weber, 1984, p. 206).

To take such a position is also to acknowledge that education is a form of moral persuasion embodying values, promoting ways of being, and teaching ethical behaviors that are less subject to the laws of empirical validation than to the rigors of democratic discourse and the difficulties of intersubjective communication.

Most significantly, early childhood specialists need to create their own research base (Caldwell, 1984). This would be a research literature that looked directly to child-care workers to define questions for investigation, to corroborate findings, and to ensure practical meaning. To create such a knowledge base, early educators would need to rely less on positivistic methods of quantitative research and more on qualitative methods employing ethnographic standards, interpretive interviews, and participant observations. The former approach appears to be antithetical to early childhood needs because it assumes a hierarchically structured research process that distances the researcher from the objects of study. On the other hand, the latter approach promotes a greater collaborative effort by both researcher and informant. Good qualitative research also respects the complexity of the teaching/ learning situation and acknowledges the whole person, purposes, and knowledge of the teacher. These are assumptions consistent with the best traditions of the field.

This is a long agenda that involves early childhood educators in examining how they think about themselves, their work, and the children they teach. It has implications for those preparing new teachers to take their places in the classrooms of the future, those already there, and those engaged in the study of teaching. Although we live in a society where rapid change is more and more taken for granted, where our lives are transformed daily by technological innovations, changes that involve qualitative shifts in how and where we seek knowledge are less quickly accomplished, if ever. But not to work toward such a change is to accept the technocratic definition of our moral and political problems and to assume that the future must repeat the past.

REFERENCES

Almy, M. (1975). *The early childhood educator at work.* New York: McGraw–Hill.

Alves, R. (1972). *Tomorrow's child.* New York: Harper & Row.

Bereiter, C., & Englemann, S. (1966). *Teaching disadvantaged children in the preschool.* Englewood Cliffs, NJ: Prentice–Hall.

Biber, B., Shapiro, E., & Wickens, D. (1971). *Promoting cognitive growth: A developmental-interaction point of view.* Washington, DC: National Association for the Education of Young Children.

Bloom, B. (1964). *Stability and change in human characteristics.* New York: Wiley.

Caldwell, B. (1984). Growth and development. *Young Children, 39*(6), 53–56.

Chamboredon, J.C. & Prevort, J. (1975). Changes in the social definition of early childhood. *Theory and Society, 3,* 331–350.

Donaldson, M. (1978). *Children's minds.* New York: Norton.

Egan, K. (1983). *Education and psychology.* New York: Teachers College Press.

Elkind, D. (1981). *Children and adolescents.* New York: Oxford University Press.

Evans, E. (1982). Curriculum models and early childhood education. In B. Spodek (Ed.), *Handbook of research in early childhood education* (pp. 107–134). New York: Free Press.

Fay, B. (1975). *Social theory and political practice.* New York: Holmes & Meier.

Gould, S. (1981). *The mismeasure of man.* New York: Norton.

Giroux, H. (1980). Critical theory and rationality in citizenship education. *Curriculum Inquiry, 10,* 329–367.

Herron, R., & Sutton-Smith, B. (1971). *Child's play.* New York: Wiley.

Hunt, J. (1961). *Intelligence and experience.* New York: Ronald.

Illich, I. (1970). *Deschooling society.* New York: Harper & Row.

Isaacs, S. (1966). *Intellectual growth in young children.* New York: Shocken.

Jersild, A. (1946). *Child development and the curriculum.* New York: Teachers College.

Katz, L. (1977). *Talks with teachers.* Washington, DC: National Association for the Education of Young Children.

Katz, M. (1971). *Class, bureaucracy and the schools.* New York: Praeger.

Kohl, H. (1967). *36 children.* New York: New American Library.

Kohlberg, L., & Mayer, R. (1972). Development as the aim of education. *Harvard Educational Review, 42,* 449–496.

Lazerson, M. (1971). Social reform and early childhood education: Some historical perspectives. In R. Anderson & H. Shane (Eds.), *As the twig is bent* (pp. 22–23). Boston: Houghton Mifflin.

Maccoby, E., & Zellner, M. (1970). *Experiments in primary education: Aspects of project Follow Through.* New York: Harcourt, Brace, Jovanovich.

Macdonald, J. (1975). Curriculum and human interests. In W. Pinar (Ed.), *Curriculum theorizing: The reconceptualists.* Berkeley, CA: McCutchan.

Merleau-Ponty, M. (1964). *The primacy of perception.* Evanston, IL: Northwestern University Press

Piaget, J. (1950). *The psychology of intelligence.* London: Routledge & Kegan Paul.

Piaget, J. (1954). *The construction of reality in the child.* New York: Basic Books.

Piaget, J. (1962). *Play, dreams and imitation in childhood.* New York: Norton.

Porter, C. (1981). *Voices from the preschool: Perspectives on early childhood educators.* Unpublished doctoral dissertation, State University of New York at Buffalo.

Rodriguez, R. (1982). *Hunger of memory.* Boston: Godine.

Seaver, J., & Cartwright, C. (1977). A pluralistic foundation for training early childhood professionals. *Curriculum Inquiry, 7,* 310–329.

Silin, J. (1982). *Protection and control: Early childhood teachers talk about authority.* Unpublished doctoral dissertation, Teachers College, New York.

Silin, J. (1985, April). *Professional knowledge and technical mindedness in early childhood education.* Paper presented at the annual meeting of the American Educational Research Association, Chicago.

Speier, M. (1976). The adult ideological viewpoint in studies of childhood. In A. Skolnick (Ed.), *Rethinking childhood* (pp. 168–186). Boston: Little, Brown.

Spodek, B. (1970). What are the sources of early childhood curriculum? *Young Children, 26,* (1), 48–58.

Spodek, B. (1984, April). *The past as prologue: Exploring the historic roots of present day concerns in early childhood education.* Paper presented at the annual meeting of the American Educational Research Association, New Orleans.

Takanishi, R. (1981). Early childhood education and research: The changing relationship. *Theory into Practice, 20,* 86–93.

Tyack, D. (1974). *The one best system.* Cambridge, MA: Harvard University Press.

Weber, E. (1984). *Ideas influencing early childhood education.* New York: Teachers College Press.

3

Early Childhood Programs in Canada

Andrew Biemiller

University of Toronto

Ellen Regan

Ontario Institute for Studies in Education

Donna Lero

University of Guelph

EARLY CHILDHOOD PROGRAMS IN CANADA

Early childhood education in Canada is concerned with the care and education of children from birth through 8 years of age. The traditional focus on day care, nursery, and kindergarten programs has expanded in recent years to include attention to the needs of infants and school-age children in primary grades (Regan, 1983). Increasingly, needs of parents and families of young children are also included in discussions of the provision of such care and education.

Within particular provinces and across the country, patterns of early care and educational provisions vary for children of different ages. For children from birth to age 5, non-parental care and education are found in numerous settings. These include day care in private homes and centers, nursery school, and public and private kindergartens. For some Canadian children ages 5 to 8, the school, through both its formal program and extra-school programs, plays a role in meeting care as well as educational needs. Extra-school programs provide supervision and activities for primary-age and some older children before and after school as well as during the lunch period. Many other children of school age spend out-of-school hours in some form of day care. Still others are on their own or in the care of an older sibling in the after-school hours.

Some form of day care or nursery programs for children from birth to age 3 is found in all provinces. However, the percentage of children receiving some kind of extra-parental care is greatest at ages 4 and 5. Provisions for these 4- and 5-year-olds vary widely among the provinces. This variation is due in part to whether or not public kindergartens are available for 5-year-olds, whether or not particular school boards have established 4-year-old kindergartens in provinces where they are a provincially supported option, and varied levels of provincial funding for day-care services. Differences within and among provinces regarding provisions for the care and education of children under the age of 8 are characteristic of Canada's complex pattern of programs and services for young children and their families.

In order to describe early childhood care and education in Canada, and to discuss some related political realities and issues, this chapter will be divided into five sections. The first section concerns the use and administration of early childhood programs, including some discussion of the cultural and linguistic realities confronted by Canadian early childhood education and the variations in programs provided by the different provinces and territories. The second describes current trends in care and educational programs, and the third examines issues presently receiving attention in provincial and federal policy discussion and in research programs. Finally, the fourth and fifth sections provide a brief review of some Canadian research concerned with the study of social and cognitive development of young children and offer a discussion of future trends in early education in Canada.

USE AND ADMINISTRATION OF EARLY CHILDHOOD PROGRAMS

As in many countries, the definition of early childhood programs in Canada has recently enlarged as need for interest in extra-home care and education have increased. Thus, all non-parental environments experienced by children from birth to age 5, as well as after-school non-parental care arrangements used by elementary schoolchildren, will be described here. Data from a 1981 survey (Statistics Canada, 1982) are now being reanalyzed by two of the present authors (Lero & Biemiller, in preparation). This survey was conducted with 18,000 families (approximately 9,000 with children from birth to age 14) or one-third of Statistics Canada's labor force study sample of February 1981. The sample is highly stratified to generate data from each province and from different regional and economic groups within provinces. (Details of sampling are available in Statistics, Canada, 1976.) The data presented below refer to care provided during the week prior to data collection.

Types of Early Childhood Settings in Canada

In Canada, as in other countries, a number of different arrangements, home- and center-based, for children are included under the rubric of early childhood education.

Center-based programs include the following types:

Day-care centers provide part- or full-day care and education for children from birth to 5 years of age, usually while parents are working. Programs generally are staffed both by teachers trained in early childhood education and by untrained staff.

Nursery schools provide part-time day-care and educational programs for children 2 to 5 years of age. Parents may or may not work. Programs usually are staffed by teachers trained in early childhood education.

Kindergartens provide part-time day-care and education programs in elementary school settings for children 4 or 5 years of age. (Programs for 4-year-olds are called junior kindergartens.) Parents may or may not work. Programs usually are staffed by certified elementary schoolteachers.

After-school programs provide care before school, at lunch, and after school for children between 4 and 12 years of age. Programs are staffed by individuals with a variety of preparations. Parents usually are working.

Home-based programs include the following types:

In-home day care describes child care provided by someone other than the child's parents. These caregivers may include siblings, other relatives, and nonrelatives. Parents usually are working.

Private-home day care encompasses child care provided in a home other than the child's. Care may be offered by relatives or nonrelatives. (This category includes both "supervised" private-home day care, in which a provincially licensed agency undertakes to monitor the quality of care, and nonsupervised private-home day care.) Parents usually are working.

Use of Early Childhood Programs by Children from Birth to 5 Years of Age

As calculated by Lero and Biemiller (in preparation), Table 1 describes, by age, percentages of children experiencing different kinds of care and education in Canada. It should be noted that use patterns such as those presented in this chapter reflect a combination of the following factors:

1. Parents' needs and desire for supplemental care as occasioned by such factors as employment, parents' enrollment in educational institutions or training programs, health and other family-need considerations, and parents' involvement in voluntary activities;
2. Parents' desire for cognitive and social enrichment experiences for their children;

Table 1   Percentage of Children 5 and Under in Full-time and Part-time Care/Education Settings

| | | | Type of Setting | | | |
Age	Number of children[a]	Parents only	Nursery school or kindergarten	Day care centers	In-home day care	Private-home day care
0–1	726,675	62.3%	b	b	17.9%	19.7%
2–3	702,785	52.6%	10.5%	8.5%	18.9%	19.1%
4	353,465	37.9%	37.6%	9.7%	18.1%	18.1%
5	355,765	17.5%	76.6%	c	20.3%	16.4%

Note. Some children use more than one setting; total percentages for age brackets are therefore more than 100. (See Table 3.)

[a] Estimated number of children in Canada, based on 1981 census. These numbers do not correspond precisely to sample estimates generated in the survey.

[b] Value less than 3.2%. Exact values cannot be reported under Statistics Canada reporting rules.

[c] Value less than 6.4%. Exact values cannot be reported under Statistics Canada reporting rules.

3. Variations in the availability and costs of the different types of care and educational programs (infant care, group day-care, nursery school, kindergarten, junior kindergarten, and after-school programs) located in different communities.

Several comments are in order with respect to the data shown in Table 1. First, when public kindergarten programs are made available in some (but not all) provinces, there is a dramatic rise in nursery-kindergarten participation at ages 4 and 5. (No distinction was drawn between nursery school and kindergarten in the interviews.) Second, as in other countries, care in home settings accounts for the vast majority of nonparental care arrangements for children age 3 and under. The percentage of children receiving some extra-parental care in homes remains quite stable through age 5. Third, once children begin to attend kindergarten or nursery school, a significant number participate in two non-parental settings. For this reason, percentages of children in various settings exceeds 100%.

Table 2 illustrates a second important aspect of extra-home care in Canada: most of this care is not "full-time" in the sense of a 9 a.m. to 5 p.m. day or longer. Only a small proportion — never exceeding 12% — is reported to receive more than 30 hours of care in one non-parental setting. Another group begins to receive care in two or more non-parental settings after turning 3 (see Table 3).

Use of two or more non-parental care settings begins to involve significant numbers of children by age 3 and becomes more common than parent-only

Table 2   Percentage of Children by Age, Hours of Extra-parental Care, and Type of Care

Age/Type of Care	Percentage of children receiving care	Hours of Care		
		Less than 20	20–29	30 or more
0–1				
Center[a]	b	b	b	b
Home[c]	37.6%	23.0%	b	11.6%
2–3				
Center	18.9%	12.0%	b	5.2%[d]
Home	38.0%	22.5%	3.6%[c]	11.9%
4				
Center	47.1%	39.8%	e	e
Home	36.2%	21.6%	e	10.0%[d]
5				
Center	81.4%	75.4%	e	e
Home	36.7%	28.5%	e	e

Note. Percentages for a particular age bracket add to more than 100 due to use of multiple care settings. (See Table 3.)

[a]"Center" care includes both day-care centers and nursery/kindergarten.

[b]Less than 3.2%. Exact values cannot be reported under Statistics Canada reporting rules.

[c]"Home" care includes both care by a nonparent in the child's home and care in another home.

[d]Percentage subject to substantial sampling error.

[e]Less than 6.4%. Exact values cannot be reported under Statistics Canada reporting rules.

Table 3   Percentage of Children 5 and Under Using Different Numbers of Care Settings

Age	Number of Care Settings			
	Parents only	Parents + 1 other setting	Parents + 2 other settings	Parents + 3 other settings
0–1	62.3%	35.1%	a	a
2–3	52.6%	39.3%	6.6%[b]	a
4	37.9%	42.6%	18.1%	c
5	17.5%	51.1%	27.1%	c

[a]Value less than 3.2%. Exact values cannot be reported under Statistics Canada reporting rules.

[b]Percentage subject to substantial sampling error.

[c]Value less than 6.4%. Exact values cannot be reported under Statistics Canada reporting rules.

care by age 5. About two-thirds of multiple-care arrangements are accounted for by nursery school or kindergarten plus home care by a nonparent or family day-care provider (see Table 4). The effects of multiple-care arrangements presently are being considered by Goelman and Pence (1984).

Use of After-school Programs by Children 6 to 14 Years of Age

Table 5 shows care arrangements outside of elementary school. Between the ages of 6 and 11, roughly 25% of children require some form of after-school care due to parents' work schedules. The type of care provided shifts dramatically with age. Two-thirds of these children receive after-school care from adults in their own or others' homes at age 6 or 7; approximately half are entirely on their own at ages 10 or 11.

Administrative and Financial Jurisdictions

As in most countries, a fundamental administrative distinction is drawn between "educational" programs, including kindergarten for 4- and 5-year-olds, and "care" programs, including nursery schools, day care, and, recently, some supervised home care. This distinction affects program guidelines, staff qualifications, and sources of financial support.

Publicly supported education. Publicly supported education is entirely the responsibility of the provinces and territories. Kindergartens are provided for 5-year-old children in all provinces except Prince Edward Island and New Brunswick. Within the provinces and territories, elected local or regional boards of education have some decision-making powers regarding curricula, books and materials, use of specialists, testing programs, and whether or not to operate kindergartens. In Quebec, Ontario, and Manitoba, local boards may also opt for junior kindergarten for 4-year-olds (Canadian Education Association, 1983). Other variations in kindergarten programs, including full-day and alternate full-day programs, will be discussed in the next section.

Table 6 shows available data on 1981 kindergarten attendance.

The Province of Alberta has a unique arrangement for kindergarten-age children. Early Childhood Services, a separate division of the provincial Ministry of Education, funds both kindergarten programs for 5-year-olds and programs for handicapped children between the ages of 3 and 8. Parents are encouraged to form cooperatives to operate kindergartens, which receive direct per capita grants. Alternatively, school boards or private schools also receive per capita grants for children enrolled in kindergarten. Enrollment in this system included 62.1% of children in Alberta in 1981. Since then, enrollment has increased to 97% of children for 1984–85. Approximately

Table 4   Combinations of Care Arrangements, Canada, 1981

Age	Parents only	Nursery School-Kindergarten			Day-care center only	In home day care only	Private home day care only	Other combinations
		Only	+ In Home day care	+ Private home day care				
0-1	62.3%	a	a	a	a	15.6%	17.2%	a
2-3	52.6%	5.3%[b]	a	a	6.0%[b]	13.0%	15.0%	4.3%[b]
4	37.9%	20.6%	7.0%[b]	7.2%[b]	c	7.2%[b]	8.4%[b]	c
5	17.5%	46.3%	13.6%	10.5%	c	c	c	7.3%

[a] Less than 3.2%. Exact values cannot be reported under Statistics Canada reporting rules.
[b] Percentage subject to substantial sampling error.
[c] Less than 6.4%. Exact values cannot be reported under Statistics Canada reporting rules.

Table 5   Percentage of Children Receiving Various Type of After-school
Care by Age

Age	Number of children[a]	After-School Care Provided by:					
		Parents only	Children on own	Sibling[b]	Other adult in child's home	Other adult in other home	School or community program
6–7	703,020	76.6%	3.4%[c]	d	5.4%	10.0%	d
8–9	718,070	75.9%	7.6%[c]	6.4%[c]	4.3%[c]	5.3%[c]	d
10–11	768,120	74.5%	12.9%	6.2%[c]	3.5%[c]	d	d
12–13	758,025	65.1%	25.9%	4.5%	d	d	d
14	394,720	56.3%	40.3%	e	e	e	e

[a]Number of children from 1981 Census. Numbers differ slightly from those generated in survey.
[b]No data available on ages of siblings.
[c]Percentage subject to substantial sampling error.
[d]Value less than 3.2%. Exact values cannot be reported under Statistics Canada reporting rules.
[e]Value less than 6.4%. Exact values cannot be reported under Statistics Canada reporting rules.

one-quarter of the programs are outside the jurisdiction of regular school boards (E. Torgunrud, personal communication, February 20, 1985).

Kindergarten programming practice does not vary systematically on a province-by-province basis. Programs are similar to kindergarten-nursery programming in the United States and Britain in emphasizing a combination of activity-based "free activity periods," outdoor play, and relatively short periods of teacher-directed activity.

Day care and nursery education.   Legally, day-care centers, nursery schools, and after-school programs come under the jurisdiction of the provinces and territories. In all cases, regulations concerning day-care nursery and after-school standards (staff–child ratios, space per child, nutrition, etc.) are under the jurisdiction of provincial and territorial ministries of social services or human resources. These groups also are responsible for social welfare services, programs for handicapped children, and other provisions. This system parallels arrangements in other Western countries.

Regulations for day-care centers vary slightly from province to province with regard to meals and snacks (typically one or two snacks and one meal for full-day programs); space (from 25 to 35 square feet per child inside, and from "safe space" to 75 square feet per child outside); and staff (1:7 for children ages 2 to 4, up to 1:15 for 5-year-olds and school-age children). Group care for infants younger than 18 months is actively discouraged (no licenses granted) in British Columbia and Saskatchewan (National Day Care Infor-

Table 6 Percentage of 4- and 5-year-old Children Attending Kindergarten

"Pre-grade 1" Enrollment[a]	Provinces with no public kindergarten		Provinces with kindergarten for 5-year-olds					Provinces with kindergarten for 5-year-olds and some 4-year-olds		
	Prince Edward Island	New Brunswick[a]	Newfoundland[a]	Nova Scotia[b]	Saskatchewan[a]	Alberta[a]	British Columbia[a]	Quebec[c]	Ontario[d]	Manitoba[e]
age 4	NA	NA	NA	NA	NA	NA	NA	7.6%	43.5%	11.1%
age 5	2.6%	4.1%	103.0%	97.1%	102.5%	62.1%	100.9%	96.6%	97.2%	88.4%

[a] Data from Statistics Canada (1983b). Includes public and private schools.
[b] Data from Ministry of Education, Nova Scotia.
[c] Data from Ministrie du Education, Government de Quebec.
[d] Data from Ministry of Education, Ontario.
[e] Data from Ministry of Education, Manitoba.

mation Centre, 1982a). Significant variations exist in provincial standards for staff qualifications. Ontario recently has instituted a requirement that one staff member in each "group" of children (2–3 staff per group) be a teacher with a degree in early childhood education from an Ontario community college or equivalent. Supervisors are mandated to have the same academic qualifications plus 2 years of experience in programs similar to that being supervised (Ministry of Social and Community Services, Ontario, 1984). In contrast, several provinces have no staff qualification requirements.

Financing of day care (including licensed or supervised private-home day care) receives support through a shared-cost arrangement (the Canada Assistance Plan), through which the federal government matches expenditures by provincial and local governments to subsidize custodial care for "needy" children. The remaining costs for capital and operating funds are shared by provinces and municipal governments and are extremely limited. Except in the case of municipal, nonprofit centers and families who qualify for day-care subsidies, operating and other costs must be borne by parents. Population and income distributions, in addition to variations in expenditure by the provinces, result in limited availability of licensed day-care spaces. Table 7 shows the average day-care expenditure per child from birth to age 5 by each province and indicates the number of children per licensed day-care space (including supervised private-home day care).

Language and Cultural Differences

The Canadian population contains a variety of different linguistic and cultural groups. The country is officially bilingual, with 68% of the population classified as Anglophone and the remainder Francophone (Statistics Canada, 1983b). However, there are a large number of people whose first language is neither English nor French. Due to large-scale immigration both before and after World War II, many other linguistic and cultural groups are present. In Toronto and Vancouver, for example, more than half the children entering school each year are not from English-speaking homes. Only a small portion of these children are Francophone. The rest are from Italian, Portuguese, Chinese, Vietnamese, East Indian, Greek, Croatian, German, Polish, Ukrainian, and other backgrounds. Thus, in many cases, early childhood programs are confronted with the problems of working with children and parents whose language is not that of the predominant population in the area.

In addition, there is a rapidly growing movement in English-speaking Canada to provide bilingual education starting in kindergarten. This instruction takes many different forms, ranging from 20-minute lessons twice a week to complete "French immersion." In 1982, more than 17% of Ontario kindergartners received some French instruction. More than a quarter of

Table 7 Expenditures and Spaces (Center and Private Home) for Day Care by Province, Canada, 1982

	Newfoundland	Prince Edward Island	Nova Scotia	New Brunswick	Quebec	Ontario	Manitoba	Saskatchewan	Alberta	British Columbia
					Province					
Expenditure per child 0–5[a]	$11.60	$34.80	$41.57	$17.57	$70.08	$101.22	$67.05	$67.05	$184.51	$87.92
Number of licensed spaces for children 0–5	533	465	3,489	2,095	23,141	43,398	6,188	2,555	16,272	12,438
Number of licensed spaces for children 6 and over	—	—	526	260	1,140	4,018	1,676	510	1,820	3,516
Expenditure per licensed space[b]	$1,261	$875	$874	$541	$1,710	$1,589	$1,498	$2,628	$2,540	$1,617
Licensed spaces as % population age 0–5: private home	0.9%	0.2%	0.1%	0.2%	0.2%	0.5%	0.9%	0.1%	0.4%	2.2%
center		3.9%	4.7%	3.2%	3.9%	5.6%	5.8%	2.5%	6.8%	3.4%

Note: Expenditures include federal contribution. Data from National Day Care Information Center (1982b).
[a] In provinces with after-school programs for children 6 and over, expenditure prorated.
[b] Expenditure per space includes expenditure for spaces for children over 5.

these were in full French immersion or in "full-day" kindergarten (9 a.m. to 3 p.m.) with half of the instruction in French (Ministry of Education, Ontario, 1982).

TRENDS IN THE CARE AND EDUCATION OF YOUNG CHILDREN IN CANADA

A number of changes — both quantitative and qualitative — are occurring in Canadian early childhood services. These include expansion of day-care centers, expansion of licensed private home care, expansion of after-school day care, exploration of the "family center" concept, and expansion of kindergartens for 4-year-olds.

Expansion of day care.   As in most Western countries, the demand in Canada for day-care services has been increasing rapidly. The percentage of married women in the labor force has increased from 35% in 1975 to 47% in 1981 for mothers of children under 6, and from 48% to 61% for mothers of school-age children (Statistics Canada, 1982). This major change in social arrangements has been accompanied by a large increase in licensed day-care services, although the increase does not begin to account for the majority of children of working parents. Currently, it is estimated that less than 15% of children under the age of 2, and 36% of children ages 2 to 5 whose parent or parents work full time are cared for in day-care centers or licensed family day-care homes. Center-based day care has increased from 27,000 spaces in 1973 to 123,000 spaces in 1983 (from 6% to 13% in total spaces). Licensed private home-care spaces have increased even more dramatically (from 1,500 in 1973 to 16,000 in 1983) and will probably continue to increase faster than center-based care (Clifford, 1984). In addition to expansion in the number of centers receiving some public funds, increased interest is evidenced by the development of policies to facilitate employers' sponsorship of day-care services.

Licensed private-home care.   The growth of private-home day care has included the development of training programs for private-home caregivers and research on the impact of various types of training (Brockman & Jackson, 1982, in preparation). Several provinces have developed or are developing provincial standards for supervised private home-care providers and/or agencies (Bates, 1984).

After-school day care.   Day care for school-age children (mostly 6 to 9 years of age) also has been increasing rapidly in the early 1980s. This increase appears to be a logical sequitur of the earlier growth of preschool day care.

More than 17,000 licensed spaces for school-age children are now available (Clifford, 1984), an increase of 4,700 in 1 year. Variation in the availability of after-school programs is evident across provinces, however. School-age programs are most prevalent in Alberta, where they are funded and coordinated by municipalities.

Many spaces are in programs established in schools with the encouragement of school boards (Canadian Education Association, 1983). In effect, many schools have vacant or extra space that, some argue, could accommodate neighborhood care and education centers for young children. This kind of accommodation is in fact taking place across Canada, as disclosed in the Canadian Education Association's 1983 survey, *Day care and the Canadian school system.* In this survey's canvass of 248 boards, 170 replies were received, with 50% of the responding boards identified as providing some kind of child-care programs in their schools. Admittedly, the survey shows that most of these programs are located in a few provinces and that the pattern of both service and accessibility within a given province varies. Data from Manitoba, for example, show that 7 out of 8 school boards report having child-care programs. In Ontario and British Columbia, such programs appear more evenly distributed among a larger number of boards.

Also according to the survey, the most frequently offered program or service is represented by the out-of-school care program. Such programs for kindergarten and elementary schoolchildren operate, as previously noted, before and after school, as well as during lunchtime, and frequently result from the cooperative effort of the school board, school administration, and parents (Canadian Education Association, 1983, p. 13). Next in order of frequency are day-care programs for children ages 2 to 5, nursery schools, day care for exceptional children, secondary school day care, infant day care (for children from birth to 2 years), drop-in centers, and language immersion programs. An idea of how these "school-housed" programs are responding to need and demand is revealed by the fact that, whereas 49 day-care and 19 nursery programs are identified by the survey, only 4 infant day-care programs are identified. Interestingly, the province of Ontario, which reports the most in-school preschool programs of this type, also has the greatest number of publicly supported 4-year-old, or junior, kindergartens.

Roles of schools and parents in providing care. The 1983 Canadian Education Association survey suggests that, as a rule, the preschool centers developing in schools are operated by community groups and agencies independent of the school. However, by suggesting in the conclusion of its survey report that "the inclusion of day care services in schools signals a new social role for the school system" (p. 36), the association sets the stage for discussion and debate within Canada regarding what the role of the school should and can be in the life of the preschool child and his or her family. The fact that community residents and parents have been instrumental in establishing these in-school centers and in determining related policies and programs also suggests a new role for parents and community in decision making affecting early education policy and practice. In this context of changing roles, some emerging attitudes and related trends are (a) the notion that early childhood education must consider family and parent as well as child needs; (b) the idea that parents are really partners in, not clients of, early childhood programs and services; and (c) the acceptance of the school as a partner in developing programs and services for preschool-age children and their families.

The family center concept.   These attitudes and trends come together in the concept and practice associated with the "family center," an approach to early care and education being considered at this time in Ontario. In theory, the family center is concerned with coordinating school and community resources to address both the development and socialization of young children and parents' need for social networks and environments that afford playmates and stimulation for their children. In practice, these centers are similar to the parent-child "drop-in" centers found in Britain, which encourage all caregivers, including those who may be providing home day care, to make use of the center program and services. Family centers developing in Ontario are different from traditional day-care centers in a number of ways, but most significantly in the attention given to parent needs, to the development of parenting/caregiving skills, and the involvement of parents in determining center policy and practice. Located in schools and elsewhere, such centers are seen as a possible answer to the schools' need to respond to family as well as child needs.

Expansion of kindergarten for 4-year-olds.   After a number of years of rapid expansion in Ontario, the junior kindergarten program now appears fairly static. Future growth depends on the willingness of local school boards to provide the program. The present state of such programs indicates that, where 4-year-old programs are not now offered, parental demand is not great. Essentially the same can be said for Quebec and Manitoba, where permissive legislation exists for 4-year-old programs but where little growth has been experienced.

ISSUES IN EARLY EDUCATION AND CARE

Two basic issues exist in Canadian early childhood education: How much and what kinds of day care should be provided? and, How much and what kinds of early childhood education should be provided? These questions appear to be overlapping. Their distinctness derives from a jurisdictional difference between the day-care and educational worlds. This jurisdictional difference is itself beginning to become an issue in public, political, and research focuses on early childhood programs.

While similar questions are being asked seriously throughout the Western world, these issues are currently receiving a good deal of political and research attention within Canada. It is quite likely that, despite the general aura of governmental restraint, early education programs will see substantial increases in financial support in the near future, thus reflecting political and public interest in the quality of care and education received by young children. In 1984-85, an internal task force on child care under the federal ministry responsible for the status of women has been reviewing research and developing position papers on various issues related to early childhood care. Furthermore, an expanded federal parliamentary task force on day care has been promised by the recently elected Conservative government.

Need for Day-care Services

Laura Johnson's *Who cares* (1977) and *Taking care* (1978) ushered in a new era of Canadian research on who is receiving care and how adequate that care appears to be. Johnson's research described day-care users and providers in Toronto. Among other things, she found that the majority of private-home care providers actually believe that, for children 3 and over, center care is preferable to care in a home setting (Johnson, 1978, p. 255). Since then, the Statistics Canada child-care survey (1982) (described in detail earlier in this chapter), a study by Lero (1981) of reasons for selecting day care, a study of school day-care options in Toronto (Neufeldt, Ferguson, Friendly, & Stephens, 1984), and a recent intensive interview study of 336 families across Canada conducted for the Federal Task Force on Child Care (Lero, Brockman, Pence, & Charlesworth, 1985) have examined day-care needs. Results of the latter study confirmed that significant needs for child-care services are not being met at the present time. In addition to regular full- and part-time care, 25% of the families interviewed required, for work-related reasons, regular evening and/or weekend care for a child under 12. Other care needs included backup arrangements on professional development days, when children are ill, and on occasions when regular child-care arrangements fall through. (Drop-in centers and centers serving the needs of shift workers are relatively rare in Canada, existing only in the largest urban areas.) The need for additional programs for children of all ages, but especially for rural children 5 to 9 years old, also was evident in this study. A new, national child-care survey by the National Day Care Research Network will provide an updated and improved picture of who needs and who uses all types of child care and early childhood programs and why. This project, under the direction of Donna Lero, has been funded by the federal government.

The present debate on day-care needs is addressed in the current report on the status of day care in Canada, which relates the number of licensed day-care spaces to the number of families in which both parents or a single parent is employed or studying full time (Clifford, 1984). This report emphasizes that, although the percentage of all children under 6 receiving licensed care is small, the percentage of those apparently in the most need who receive such care is much greater. Unfortunately, the data analyses on which such findings are based still leave many questions unanswered. Full-day spaces are frequently used by more than one child on a part-time basis; families requiring care in evening hours or to match shift work patterns are not considered (see Table 8).

These data suggest that the care needs of approximately a third to a quarter of preschool children, but much smaller percentages of infants and school-age children, may presently be being met by the existing provincial child-care systems. (These percentages will vary markedly across provinces, as indicated in Table 7.) The gap between services offered and needed is being felt politically, as evidenced by discussion of the issue during the recent national election and the promised establishment by the new government of a parliamentary task force on day care.

Effects of Day Care on Children

While research and interest concerning needs and reasons for child care continue to grow, research on the underlying question of the effects of extra-home care on children and families has just begun to have a role in the Canadian debate. At present, one major Canadian study has attempted to examine

Table 8   Percentage of Canadian Children in *Licensed* Child Care Settings (Including Centers and Private Home Care) Canada, 1983

	Age of Children		
Parents' Employment Status	Under 2	2–5	6–13
Mothers in labor force	5.4%	16.1%	1.3%
Full-time working parents	13.6%	35.7%	2.5%
Full-time working parents + students	12.5%	32.6%	2.3%
Full-time working parents + students + one or single parent working 20–29 hours a week	10.1%	26.0%	1.8%

Note. Data from *Status of day care in Canada, 1983,* by H. Clifford, 1984, Ottawa: Health and Welfare Canada.

the experiences of children in different types of care settings and to assess some of the short-term consequences associated with them (Goelman & Pence, 1984; Pence & Goelman, 1982). This study emphasizes extensive observational methods. Based on Bronfenbrenner's human ecology framework (Bronfenbrenner, 1979), the Pence and Goelman (1982) study examines the interaction between social, familial, and individual aspects of the day-care experience. The investigation includes measures of the cognitive, language, and social development of children in licensed center day care, licensed private-home care, and unlicensed private-home day care. Recent findings in the United States suggest that early experiences can have demonstrable effects many years later (Lazar & Darlington, 1982). (A difficulty in designing such studies is the fact that use of early child-care arrangements probably indicates a continuing family situation that will be different from that experienced in homes where only one parent works or where one parent is home during children's after-school hours.)

Jacobs's study of privacy seeking (1980a) and review of privacy behavior and day-care environments (1980b) indicate that preschool children need and use privacy to develop personal autonomy and that privacy may play a role in information processing, self-evaluation, and emotional release. She makes practical recommendations based on this research for various ways of providing privacy within day-care environments (Jacobs, 1980b, pp. 130–131).

Two studies have examined the consequences of day-care and nursery school experience for elementary schoolchildren. McKinnon (1982) has indicated that middle-class children who attended nursery school, Montessori school, or no preschool were reported by parents and teachers to show similar progress on physical, self-help, social, academic, and communication scales. Innerd (1982) has collected records on all children entering the Windsor, Ontario, public school system. He plans to use formal assessments conducted by the school system to examine outcomes as a function of preschool experience.

Effects of Multiple Care Settings

Increasing numbers of children of 5 years of age and under are found in some form of extra-home care, and a growing number of 4- and 5-year-olds are spending time in two extra-home settings (i.e., some form of day care and kindergarten; see Table 3). In fact, some of the major concerns and issues surrounding early childhood education policy and practice in Canada today derive from such multiple care and educational experiences. Specific issues relate to the continuity of children's experiences in multiple settings, parental expectations for different settings, and effects on children of simultaneous exposure to provisions in different settings. Obviously, these sets of issues embrace a number of concerns, including program emphasis or purpose in different settings, expectations for children in different settings, the effects on peer socialization of moving from one setting to another, and other social and physical demands on children (e.g., fatigue).

Financing of Day Care

The financing of day care remains a contentious issue. The "motherhood" issues of who should raise children and who should pay for care and education are much debated. Should families who choose to have a parent at home subsidize families who do not (and in many cases cannot)? Should individuals and families without children at home help pay for the care of others' children, as they have long helped pay for their education? One thrust in Ontario has been provision of government funding for the expansion of day-care services that, once in place, will be self-supporting.

School boards in most provinces have begun to make surplus facilities available for day-care operations (Canadian Education Association, 1983). Presently, Quebec is the only province that allows school boards to operate day-care services directly for a fee. Day-care fees are tax deductible up to $2,000 per child. (This arrangement helps wealthy parents considerably more than those who are less well-off.) Whether any major changes in the present patchwork funding of day-care services by parents, all levels of government, and, to some extent, day-care providers (through very low salaries) will occur is a moot point. It seems probable that the gradual growth of care arrangements — both licensed and unlicensed — will continue. A dramatic change (e.g., making funds available for child care to a larger income group, a substantially larger child-care deduction on taxes, a significantly increased role of the educational system in day care) may come from the current federal task force or from one or more provinces. However, we anticipate more gradual developments.

Teacher Training

The quality of child-adult interaction in preschool and early primary settings has been the focal point of Brophy's assessment of the interaction between adults and special needs (developmentally delayed) and nonspecial needs preschoolers (Brophy, 1985; Brophy & Reinsoo, 1983; Brophy & Stone–Zukowski, 1984). Brophy (1985) concludes from these studies that teachers may need specific new techniques for assisting verbal and communication development in low-verbal and nonverbal children. Miezitis, Gotlieb, Steele, & Pierre–Perone (1985) studied use of feedback to student teachers as an approach to modifying interactions with particular children.

Interest in teacher education/caregiver training and concerns related to the professional development of in-service teachers have resulted both in exploratory studies and in the development of training programs. Doucet, Betsalet–Presser, & Donommes–Roitaille's (1984) concern with identifying teacher's professional development needs was the focus of an exploratory study involving teacher interviews. In the process of developing a training program for family day-care providers, Brockman investigated the relative effectiveness of three training models in improving the quality of caregiving (Brockman & Jackson, 1982; Brockman & Jackson, in preparation). Preliminary analysis of Brockman's study indicates that, as compared with caregivers in two control groups, caregivers who participated in 1-week direct training programs improved the observed quality of their interactions with infants. Although samples were small (nine caregivers in each of four groups), a second interesting finding was that only one of the participants in the short training courses ceased caregiving within a year, while six left from the control groups (L. Brockman, personal communication, October 24, 1985).

King–Shaw and Unruh (1984) have conducted a survey of preservice preparation for kindergarten teachers in faculties of education across Canada. They report that, despite the growing interest in early education, preparation of kindergarten teachers remains largely a sideline in teacher education institutions. Their report also contains teachers' views on improving preservice and in-service programs for teachers.

Early Identification

Early identification of learning disabilities in kindergarten has been a subject of policy concern in Ontario for a number of years. Research conducted by O'Bryan in Windsor, Ontario (O'Bryan, 1976) led to the view that children who would develop learning disabilities could be identified at the senior kindergarten level. Follow-up research in third grade confirms that a series of test batteries and teacher ratings provides reasonably accurate predictions of school performance (O'Bryan, 1981). The follow-up study also indicated that such identification procedures carried out with junior kindergarten children were not effective and that interventions subsequent to kindergarten were not related to the identification procedures. A later study by Davidson, Silverman, and Hughes (1981) of provincially mandated early identification procedures in Ontario found that a "lack of clarity about purpose was frequently apparent within boards, and lack of consistency [existed] between boards with regard to goals, procedures, and techniques" (p. iii).

Continuity from Ages 4 to 8

The issue of continuity of programming between kindergarten and the early primary grades is being examined in both Ontario and Alberta. In Ontario, the Early Primary Education Project conducted by the Ministry of Education is currently examining programs for children ages 4 to 8. Particular emphasis is being given to reviewing program content, maintaining continuity in programming from kindergarten through the early primary years, and improving coordination between different agencies (e.g., education, day care, municipal supports, etc.) dealing with children in this age range and their parents. This project is a response to both the ministry's own finding that the nature of programming provided in kindergarten and first grade differs to an undesirable degree in terms of child-chosen versus direct instruction (Ministry of Education, Ontario, 1983) and the findings and recommendations of a study of education in Ontario (LaPierre, 1980). Among the recommendations of the latter study is one supporting the creation of family centers concerned with providing a full range of care and education services for children 0–8 and their families. This concept of the family center differs from that described earlier in that it would essentially replace the early primary school years.

In Alberta, a recent study examined "articulation" between kindergarten and first grade (Pain, 1984). Defining high articulation as including (a) continuity of experience between kindergarten and first grade in methods and philosophy, (b) opportunity for kindergarten and first-grade children to interact, (c) involvement of parents in the program, and (d) communication and joint planning among teachers, this study contrasted high- versus low-articulation first grades by examining data derived from observations and interviews with teachers and principals. High-articulation teachers placed more emphasis on individual development. Self-confidence, self-direction, and enjoyment of learning were stressed by these teachers. More self-selection and opportunities to proceed at the child's pace were permitted, as was more helping among children. Unfortunately, this study did not include examination of measurable effects on children, either in terms of observed behavior or developed abilities.

Compensatory Education

Compensatory education has been of interest in Canada at least since the opening of the first kindergarten for 4-year-olds in Toronto in 1940. Beneficial effects for deprived and non-English-speaking children were an assumption in the development of 4-year-old kindergartens in Ontario in the 1960s. More recently, demonstration projects by Palmer (1966) and especially Wright (1983) have emphasized the potential of preschool education to have some compensatory impact on children from poor socioeconomic backgrounds. Wright's work is of interest because it focuses on an urban Canadian population differing in composition from comparable populations in the United States, and does not involve a parent component. She found compensatory effects up to 3 years after program participation. On the other hand, research by Fowler (1978) on infant day-care programs failed to show any significant effects of compensatory education.

Compensatory programs for native (American Indian) children have been a related concern. The Central Regina (Saskatchewan) Early Learning Center, established in September 1977, is an early intervention program for disadvantaged preschoolers from 3 to 5 years of age. This program encourages a high level of parental involvement and seeks to "enhance the well-being and self-determination of the family unit within the community" (Deines, 1981, p. 131). With few exceptions, the children and parents involved are of native origin, and the first language of most participants is English. Although the program emphasizes the development of basic skills, attention is given to promoting pride in the children's and parent's cultural heritage.

Mayfield (1983) describes a project concerned with supporting infant growth and development through training programs for parents and community residents on a reserve in British Columbia. This adult training program combined modern ideas of child development with traditional native teachings. Although the sample sizes are too small to draw definite conclusions, Mayfield's evaluation of the program suggests a reduction of kindergarten "failures" and an increase in the number of children classified as normal on the Denver Developmental Screening Test.

Full-day Kindergarten

The availability of classroom space and teachers, combined with the growing need for child care and interest in the beneficial effects of early education, has led to experiments with full-day kindergarten programs (9 a.m. to 3:30 p.m.). Biemiller (1983) compared children who had attended full-day kindergarten in two rural counties with comparable children who had attended half-day or alternate full-day kindergarten. No differences in academic skills or teacher ratings of temperament and self-direction were found either in kindergarten or in second grade. Bates, Deeth, Wright, and Vernon (in press) examined the impact of full-day kindergarten on deprived urban children. Again, no important differences were reported.

In addition, full-day kindergartens are used in Ottawa, Toronto, Montreal, and elsewhere in conjunction with French-immersion classes. French is used for the afternoon component of the kindergarten program and full time thereafter. Reports by Avid (1979, 1980) compared English-speaking, Greek-speaking, and French-speaking children in French-immersion kindergarten. Depending on the measure used, results indicated either that English- and Greek-speaking children made similar progress in French or that Greek-speaking children made more progress. Attendance in French-speaking schools facilitated progress.

CANADIAN RESEARCH RELATED TO EARLY CHILDHOOD EDUCATION

Canadian researchers also are involved in the study of social and cognitive development of children in preschool settings and in investigations of the problems of special-needs children. Research related to social development includes the extensive work of Rubin, Ross, and colleagues on peer relationships and social skills (Rubin & Ross, 1982); Jacobs's (1980b) study of social networks and peer relations among preschool children; and the work of White and her colleagues (Mendelson & White, 1983; White, Mauro, & Spindler, 1983) focusing on how children develop ideas about sex role, ethnic identity, and body image.

Weininger's (1979) analysis of the functions of play has influenced both teachers and policy development. For example, his concerns about freedom for exploration and play have been reflected in the recent Ministry of Education, Ontario (1985) document *Shared discovery.*

Studies by Case and his colleagues (Case, 1985, chap. 8; Case & Khanna, 1981) have emphasized the development of intellectual capacity during the preschool years. Using a theory combining Piagetian and information-processing conceptions of cognitive growth, these researchers have examined the development of storytelling, social problem solving, solutions to balance beam problems, and other aspects of mental growth in the preschool years.

The Laboratory of Human Ethology in Montreal, under the direction of Fred Strayer, has been involved in a long-term study of social development in children ages 1 to 5. Recent reports from the laboratory have examined the growth of dominance and affiliative hierarchies (Strayer & Trudel, 1984), emergence of same-sex preferences (LaFreniere, Strayer, & Gauthier, 1984), and conflicts involving groups of three children (Strayer & Noel, in press). While Strayer and his colleagues have not focused specifically on early childhood issues, their findings present a wealth of information about the behavior of young children in day-care settings. An overview of his methods and of their generalizability over a number of different settings appears in Strayer (1980).

An important aspect of much research currently under way in Canada is the development of instruments for and methods of studying young children and their environments. Design and evaluation of measures are critical components of Brockman and Jackson's (in preparation) study of family day-care settings. Krasnor and Rubin (1981, 1983) have been concerned with developing measures of social problem solving. Nash (1981) has developed a sequence of teacher-observable criteria for comparing children's classroom skills in a kindergarten program with monthly progress norms. Biemiller and Morley (in press) have developed a video and interview technique for looking at children's self-direction, and Doucet et al. (1984) and Regan (in press) have been concerned with refining interview techniques used in exploring teacher perceptions and beliefs.

THE FUTURE FOR EARLY CHILDHOOD RESEARCH AND PROGRAMS

Future early childhood research and programming are likely to be influenced by social concerns and by public and professional perceptions of the care and educational needs of young children and their families. Certainly, increasing attention to family and child needs at both policy-making and practical levels is characteristic of the current early childhood scene in Canada. In contrast to the traditional concerns with parent involvement in supporting child development and learning, current perceptions of such involvement include the participation of parents in policy discussions to determine the nature of care and education in early childhood settings (Canadian Education Association, 1983; Pain, 1984). As parents assume a greater partnership with early childhood professionals, social agencies within communities likewise are becoming more involved in policy development and programming. One positive feature of the increase in groups and agencies concerned has been the effort, in some communities, to develop better understanding among the institutions involved. This trend is especially evident in communities where communication and cooperation have been established between schools and other community agencies.

A significant outcome of broad-based participation in early childhood care and education has been the development of a number of alternatives to more traditional provisions. In fact, the variety of options within Canada and the number of individuals, community groups, and social agencies involved in provision is also characteristic of the current situation. Although this variety of options is not necessarily available to most families, the development of alternatives to meet varying child and family needs is a decided trend.

From a research perspective, this trend is likely to promote increased systematic study of program variations in different settings as well as study of the effects of different and/or multiple-care settings and education in the early years. The study of early childhood programming and its effects is increasingly concerned with developing means for describing the process of what in fact goes on in various settings (e.g., Goelman & Pence, 1984; Strayer, 1980; Strayer & Trudel, 1984) and with determining parents' perceptions of satisfaction with particular care and educational provisions (e.g., Lero, 1981; Lero et al., 1985; Statistics Canada, 1982).

Finally, the early childhood field in Canada is characterized by growing recognition of the need to conceptualize the care and education of children ages 4 through 8 in ways that promote a continuum of experience and easy transitions from preschool to kindergarten to primary grades. In addition to an increase in dialogue among the individuals and agencies involved, another response to this need is seen in proposals for innovations in the training of teachers and other early childhood professionals. Specific proposals address more specialized early childhood education training for primary grade teachers and more training for all professionals to promote the skills and understanding needed to work effectively with parents, community workers, and agencies.

In summary, Canadian research and policy analysis related to early childhood education and care are rapidly approaching a critical mass. Descriptive research studies are documenting the large percentage of children experiencing early childhood care. More is being learned about children's care and educational histories; this information is in turn attracting interest in examining such issues as the quality components essential to care in each type of setting; continuity between programs and experiences; and the consequences of alternative preschool experiences on children's academic, social, and personal development. Increased public demand for day care, early childhood education, family resource programs, and after-school services also is contributing to a sense of urgency in this area. In the years to come, we might anticipate not only additional programs, but also exciting research on alternative models for providing care and education to meet the diverse needs of Canadian children and their families.

REFERENCES

Avid, E. (1979). *A comparison of early immersion and classes d'accueil programs at the kindergarten level.* (ERIC Document Reproduction Service No. ED 225 372)

Avid, E. (1980). *Starting French in kindergarten: The effects of program, mother tongue, and other linguistic experience on second language development.* (ERIC Document Reproduction Service No. ED 225 368)

Bates, H.B. (1984). *Day care standards in Canada.* Ottawa: Canada National Task Force on Child Care.

Bates, J., Deeth, M., Wright, E., & Vernon, J. (in press). *The full-day kindergarten study.* Toronto: Ministry of Education, Ontario.

Biemiller, A. (1983). *A longitudinal study of thriving, average and non-thriving children from kindergarten to grade two.* Toronto: Ministry of Education, Ontario.

Biemiller, A., & Morley, E. (in press). Explorations in self direction. In E. Regan & A. Biemiller (Eds.), *Studies of teacher's perceptions and practices* (pp. 326–367). Toronto: Ministry of Education, Ontario.

Brockman, L., & Jackson, E.L. (1982). *Facilitating social interaction in an integrated setting: A manual for caregivers.* Winnipeg: University of Manitoba.

Brockman, L., & Jackson, E. (in preparation). *Experimental training programs for family day care providers.* Winnipeg: University of Manitoba.

Bronfenbrenner, U. (1979). *The ecology of human development.* Cambridge MA: Harvard University Press.

Brophy, K. (1985, April). *Teacher interaction with special needs and non-special needs pre-schoolers.* Paper presented at the meeting of the Society of Research in Child Development, Toronto, Canada.

Brophy, K., & Reinsoo, E. (1983, June). *The non-verbal communication of special needs and comparison of toddlers and preschoolers.* Paper presented at the meeting of the Canadian Society for the Study of Education, Vancouver.

Brophy, K., & Stone–Zukowski, D. (1984). Social and play behaviors of special needs and non-special needs children. *Early Child Development and Care, 13,* 137–154.

Canadian Education Association. (1983). *Day care and the Canadian school system.* Toronto: Author.

Case, R. (1985). *Intellectual development: A systematic reinterpretation.* New York: Academic.

Case, R., & Khanna, F. (1981). The missing link: Stages in children's progression from sensorimotor to logical thought. In K.W. Fischer (Ed.), New directions for child development (Vol. 12, pp. 21–32). San Francisco: Jossey–Bass.

Clifford, H. (1984). *Status of day care in Canada, 1983.* Ottawa: Health and Welfare Canada.

Davidson, I., Silverman, H., & Hughes, M. (1981). *Learning abilities: Identification and intervention practices.* Toronto: Ministry of Education, Ontario.

Deines, A. (1981). *A review of early childhood education programs* (Vol. 2). Regina: Saskatchewan Education Policy, Planning and Special Projects.

Doucet, E., Betsalet–Presser, R., & Denommes–Roitaille, N. (1984, June). *Exploratory study on professional needs and the early childhood teacher's professional development.* Paper presented at the annual conference of the Canadian Society for the Study of Education, Guelph, Ontario.

Fowler, W. (1978). *Day care and its effects on early development.* Toronto: O.I.S.E. Press.

Goelman, H., & Pence, A. (1984, June). *The ecology of day care in one Canadian city. Year one of the Victoria day care project.* Paper presented at the meeting of the Canadian Society for the Study of Education, Guelph, Ontario.

Innerd, W. (1982, June). *The long-term effects of pre-school experiences.* Paper presented at the meeting of the Canadian Society for the Study of Education, Ottawa.

Jacobs, E. (1980a, August). *Intrusion and aggression in the preschool setting.* Paper presented at the World Conference for OMEP, Quebec City, Canada.

Jacobs, E. (1980b). The privacy behavior of preschool children: Mechanisms and functions in the day care environment. In P. Wilkinson (Ed.), *In celebration of play* (pp. 119–134). London: Croom Helm.

Johnson, L. (1977). *Who cares.* Toronto: Social Planning Council of Metropolitan Toronto.

Johnson, L. (1978). *Taking care.* Toronto: Social Planning Council of Metropolitan Toronto.

King–Shaw, E., & Unruh, W. (1984, June). *A survey of early childhood education in Ontario.* Paper presented at the annual conference of the Canadian Society for the Study of Education, Guelph, Ontario.

Krasnor, L., & Rubin, K. (1981). Assessment of social problem solving in young children. In T. Merluzzi, C. Glass, & M. Genest (Eds.), *Cognitive assessment.* New York: Guilford.

Krasnor, L., & Rubin, K. (1983). Preschool social problem solving attempts and outcomes in naturalistic interaction. *Child Development, 54,* 1545–1558.

LaFreniere, P., Strayer, F.F., & Gauthier, R. (1984). The emergence of same-sex affiliative preferences among preschool peers: A developmental/ethological perspective. *Child Development, 55,* 1958–1965.

LaPierre, L. (1980). *To herald a child.* Toronto: Commission of Inquiry into the Education of the Young Child.

Lazar, I., & Darlington, K. (1982). Lasting effects of early education: A report from the Consortium for Longitudinal Studies. *Monographs of the Society for Research in Child Development, 47*(2–3, Serial No. 195).

Lero, D. (1981). *Day care factors influencing parents' preferences for and use of alternative child care arrangements for preschool children.* University of Guelph, Ontario.

Lero, D., & Biemiller, A. (in preparation). *Childcare arrangements in Canada, 1981.* University of Guelph, Ontario.

Lero, D., Brockman, L., Pence, A., & Charlesworth, M. (1985). *Parents' needs, preferences, and concerns about child care: Case studies of 336 Canadian families.* Ottawa: Canada National Task Force on Child Care.

Mayfield, M. (1983, June). *Longitudinal evaluation of a Canadian program for the native infant and family: An interim report.* Paper presented at the meeting of the Canadian Society for the Study of Education, Vancouver, British Columbia.

McKinnon, J. (1982). *A comparative study of the effects of preschool education on middle class children.* (ERIC Document Reproduction Service No. ED 220 179)

Meizitis, S., Gotlieb, H., Steele, J., & Pierre–Perone, K. (in press). Student-teachers' perceptions: Assessment and intervention. In E. Regan & A. Biemiller (Eds.), *Studies of teachers' perceptions and practices* (pp. 215–291). Toronto: Ministry of Education, Ontario.

Mendelson, B.K., & White, D. (1983). Relation between body-esteem and self-esteem of obese and normal children. *Perceptual and Motor Skills, 54,* 899–905.

Ministry of Education, Ontario. (1982). *Education statistics Ontario, 1982.* Toronto: Author.

Ministry of Education, Ontario. (1983). Report of the junior kindergarten, kindergarten, grade one task force. *Provincial Review Report, 1,* 1–13.

Ministry of Education, Ontario. (1985). *Shared discovery.* Toronto: Author.

Ministry of Social and Community Services, Ontario. (1984). *Standards for day nurseries.* Toronto: Author.

Nash, C. (1981). *Early childhood identification through observation: A diagnostic teaching kit.* Toronto: Collier-MacMillan Canada.

National Day Care Information Centre. (1982a). *Provincial day care requirements.* Ottawa: Health and Welfare, Canada.

National Day Care Information Centre. (1982b). *Provincial funding of day care services.* Ottawa: Health and Welfare, Canada.

Neufeldt, M., Ferguson, E., Friendly, M., & Stephens, M. (1984). *Choices, options and directions for school-age child care.* Toronto: Metro Toronto Children's Advisory Group.

O'Bryan, K.G. (1976). *The Windsor early identification project.* Toronto: Ministry of Education, Ontario.

O'Bryan, K.G. (1981). *The Windsor early identification project revisited.* Toronto: Ministry of Education, Ontario.

Pain, K. (1984). *Articulation linkages. Children and parents in early basic education.* Edmonton: Planning Services, Alberta Education.

Palmer, J. (1966). *The effects of junior kindergarten on achievement.* Toronto: Toronto Board of Education, Research Department.

Pence, A., & Goelman, H. (1982). *The ecology of day care.* Victoria: University of Victoria.

Regan, E. (1983). Early childhood education in, *The Canadian encyclopedia,* Edmonton: Hurtig.

Regan, E. (in press). Exploring teacher's perceptions and beliefs. In E. Regan & A. Biemiller (Eds.), *Studies of teachers' perceptions and practices* (pp. 1–53). Toronto: Ministry of Education, Ontario.

Rubin, K., & Ross, H. (Eds.). (1982). *Peer relationships and social skills.* The Hague: Springer–Verlag.

Statistics Canada. (1976). *Methodology of the Canadian labour force survey.* Ottawa: Ministry of Supply and Services, Canada.

Statistics Canada. (1982). *Initial results from the 1981 survey of child care arrangements.* (Labour Force Survey Research Paper No. 31, Cat. 8-3100-532.) Ottawa: Ministry of Supply and Services, Canada.

Statistics Canada. (1983a). *Education in Canada: 1983*. (Cat. 81-229.)

Statistics Canada. (1983b). *1981 Census of Canada: Population, mother tongue, official language and home language*. (Cat. 92-910.) Ottawa: Ministry of Supply and Services, Canada.

Strayer, F. (1980). Social ecology of the preschool peer group. In W.A. Collins (Ed.), *Minnesota symposia on child psychology* (Vol. 13, pp. 165-196). Hillsdale, NJ: Erlbaum.

Strayer, F., & Noel, J.M. (in press). Triadic conflict among young children: An ethological study of prosocial and antisocial aggression. In C. Zahn-Wexler (Ed.), *Altruism and aggression: Socio- and socio-biological origins*. New York: Cambridge University Press.

Strayer, F., & Trudel, M. (1984). Developmental changes in the nature and function of social dominance among young children. *Ethology and Sociobiology, 5,* 279-295.

Weininger, O. (1979). *Play and education: The basic tool for early childhood learning*. Springfield, IL: Charles G. Thomas.

White, D., Mauro, K., & Spindler, J. (1983). La formation des préjugés liés à l'apparence physique chez les jeunes enfants d'age préscolaire. *Appresentage et Socialisation, 6.*

Wright, M. (1983). *Compensatory education: A Canadian approach*. Ypsilanti, MI: High/Scope Press.

4

Problems in Children's Peer Relations: A Broadening Perspective

Christine B. Burton

Florida State University

INTRODUCTION

Social relationships all have their ups and downs. Conflict within relationships can in fact be a healthy process, strengthening the bond between social partners (Rubin, 1980) and teaching important social skills such as communication and compromise (Asher, Renshaw, & Hymel, 1982). Relationships with peers constitute a central element in children's social lives (Hartup, 1983), and most children are able to cope successfully with the problems that inevitably arise within these relationships. Friends may quarrel, but in most cases their disagreements are resolved and forgotten. Even when children's friendships do end, however, new relationships usually soon begin. Thus, despite occasional setbacks, the majority of children find their peer relationships to be an enduring source of both satisfaction (e.g., Asher, Hymel, & Renshaw, 1984) and security (e.g., Schwartz, 1972).

At the same time, there are a number of children for whom peer relations spell only persistent trouble. Researchers have found that about 5 to 10% of elementary schoolchildren are unable to acquire and maintain friendships with other members of their classes (Asher & Renshaw, 1981). These children who lack friends should be of critical concern to parents and teachers alike. The children clearly miss out on many of the good times that close friends and associates are able to share. Perhaps more importantly, they also miss out on crucial social learnings (Combs & Slaby, 1977). Indeed, children who experience serious problems with peer relationships are likely to develop additional adjustment problems in later life, including academic and behavioral problems during adolescence (e.g., Roff, Sells, & Golden, 1972) and mental health problems during adulthood (e.g., Cowen, Pederson, Babigian, Izzo, & Trost, 1973).

This chapter examines recent advances in knowledge about children with peer relationship problems. Two specific developments are described: (1) an emerging recognition of the differences that exist between socially *rejected* versus *neglected* children; and (2) a growing appreciation for children's perspectives on their own social situations. It has only been within the past few years that researchers have conducted systematic studies to explore either of these issues.

The chapter is divided into four parts. The first section focuses on sociometric methods for identifying low-status children who may be experiencing difficulties in peer relations. The second section describes findings from recent studies on the behavioral correlates of children's peer status. In both the first and second sections, evidence is presented to support the distinction between rejected and neglected children. The third section of the chapter surveys new information on the link between peer status and children's subjective sense of well-being. This information documents the importance of looking beyond observable aspects of children's social problems to consider the perceptions and feelings of the children themselves. The chapter then ends with a discussion of techniques that have been found to be effective for helping children overcome problems in their peer relations.

SOCIOMETRIC ASSESSMENT OF PEER RELATIONSHIP PROBLEMS

Sociometric methodology has been used widely to study children's peer relations (for reviews, see Asher & Hymel, 1981; Hymel, 1983a). By providing information about the relative status of peer group members, sociometric methods have enabled researchers to identify children who are having difficulties in establishing relationships with peers. Such low-status children are considered to be socially and psychologically at risk, so their clear-cut identification is critical (Asher & Hymel, 1981; Putallaz & Gottman, 1982).

The most commonly used sociometric method has been the peer nomination method. Within this approach, positive nominations (e.g., "Which classmates do you like the most?") measure how much children are liked by their peers, while negative nominations (e.g., "Which classmates do you like the least?") measure how much children are disliked or rejected. Most studies of children's peer relations have been limited to the use of positive nomination measures. Children's social status has thus been typically defined in terms of how much the children are liked, or how popular they are among their peers (Asher & Hymel, 1981; Asher & Renshaw, 1981; Gronlund, 1959).

Although researchers have typically relied upon positive nominations to determine social status, it was acknowledged long ago that this practice actually confounds two distinct types of low-status children: those who are *rejected* and those who are *neglected* (see Northway, 1944; Thompson & Powell, 1951). Rejected children are not liked and are actively disliked by peers; neglected children are simply not noticed, or overlooked (Asher &

Hymel, 1981). Traditionally, both rejected and neglected children have been classified under the single label of the unpopular child (Meichenbaum, Bream, & Cohen, in press).

Evidence to support the distinction between rejected and neglected status has accumulated over the years, coming first from clinical observations (Bronfenbrenner, 1944; Northway, 1944, 1946) and later from more objective analyses of sociometric data. Empirical comparisons of children's positive and negative sociometric nomination scores have shown the scores to be only slightly negatively related (Gottman, 1977; Moore & Updegraff, 1964; Roff et al., 1972), if related at all (Goldman, Corsini, & deUrioste, 1980; Hartup, Glazer, & Charlesworth, 1967). This suggests that negative sociometric nominations do contribute unique information about children's social status which cannot be obtained through positive nominations alone (Moore & Updegraff, 1964). Specifically, negative nominations provide a methodology for subclassifying low-status children into those who are rejected and those who are neglected.

Researchers now tend to agree that the rejected–neglected distinction is essential to the precise delineation of children's social status categories. An interest in sorting out the unique problems of rejected versus neglected children has therefore been a guiding force behind recent investigations into children's peer relationship problems. Underlying such interest is a desire to enhance our ability to intervene in ways that meet the children's individual needs. Even more basic is a desire to determine whether rejected and neglected children each require intervention. While it is true that both types of low-status children fail to establish close relationships with classroom peers, it is not clear whether the two groups are equally at risk because of this fact. Research bearing on these issues is discussed in subsequent sections of the chapter.

Before proceeding, though, a final comment is in order. There is as yet little empirical documentation of the effects that sociometric testing has on children and their social interactions. Without this knowledge, many researchers and practitioners remain skeptical about using sociometric procedures. In the only research available, Hayvren and Hymel (1984) found that preschool children did not change their behavior toward either liked or disliked peers as a result of sociometric interviews, including the administration of negative nomination measures. The children did not, in fact, discuss their negative sociometric choices at all when they returned to the classroom playgroup. These are encouraging findings which support claims that the benefits of sociometric assessment outweigh the risks (see Asher, 1983; Moore, 1967). Nonetheless, more research is needed if we are to understand fully the consequences of sociometric testing for both preschool and school-age children. A particularly important research direction would be the comparative study of the effects of individual versus group administration procedures. Although group procedures are often used, it seems likely that any potential negative effects of sociometric measures would be strongest when children respond in a group setting. Furthermore, as Hayvren and Hymel (1984) noted, it will also be important to examine the impact that sociometric testing has on children's self-perceptions and their affective states.

THE BEHAVIORAL CORRELATES OF PEER RELATIONSHIP PROBLEMS

Sociometric measures are useful for the identification of children who are having difficulties in peer relations. Sociometric measures provide no information, however, to aid in identifying the origin of children's social problems, or in detecting the factors that currently maintain the problems (Putallaz & Gottman, 1982). This requires more extensive investigation.

Although several explanations have been advanced to account for low social status, a behavioral perspective has predominated (Asher & Hymel, 1981; Putallaz & Gottman, 1981, 1982; Renshaw & Asher, 1982). The social-skill deficit model proposed by Asher and his colleagues (Asher & Renshaw, 1981) describes this perspective in its most fully articulated form. According to the model, individual skillfulness is the crucial determinant of children's peer status. More specifically, it is hypothesized that low-status children are prevented from establishing effective peer relationships due to their own lack of social skills (Asher & Renshaw, 1981). The primary goal of research based on the social-skill model is the identification of skills that differentiate low-status children from children who are relatively more successful in their peer relations. An underlying assumption is that once the critical skills are identified, a "correctional process" (Putallaz & Gottman, 1982, p. 2) can be implemented to help the low-status children.

The literature on the social-skill correlates of sociometric status has focused primarily on children's overt behavioral styles (Asher & Renshaw, 1981). Since the 1930s, researchers have repeatedly attempted to characterize the behaviors of low- versus high-status children (for reviews, see Asher & Hymel, 1981; Asher, Oden, & Gottman, 1977; Asher et al., 1982). In general, low-status children have been found to exhibit less positive and less effective styles of social interaction than their higher-status peers. Until recently, however, few studies had been designed to assess behavioral differences between the two types of low-status children.

As indicated, researchers have begun to recognize the necessity of differentiating between rejected and neglected status. Accordingly, they have applied the rejected–neglected distinction in new studies on the behavioral styles of low-status children (Carlson, Lahey, & Neeper, 1984; Coie, Dodge, & Coppotelli, 1982; Coie & Kupersmidt, 1983; Dodge, 1983; Dodge, Coie, & Brakke, 1982; French & Waas, 1985; Green, Vosk, Forehand, & Beck, 1981).

The results of these studies are reviewed next. In each of the studies under review, status groupings have been accomplished through the combined use of positive and negative nomination sociometric measures.

Peer and Teacher Assessments of Low-status Children

Researchers have used a variety of behavioral assessment techniques to study the interaction styles of rejected and neglected children. A number of studies have involved the use of peer and teacher assessments. Other studies have been based on more direct observational methods.

Gronlund and Anderson (1957) exemplified the use of peer assessments in their comparison of socially rejected, neglected, and accepted junior high school students. This represents one of the first studies to focus separately on the characteristics of rejected versus neglected children. In the study, students nominated peers who best fit a variety of personal characteristics. The mean scores for each status group were then compared across the list of characteristics. Rejected students received the most nominations for being restless, talkative, and *not* likable, while neglected students received nominations only for being quiet. Accepted children were nominated the most for being cheerful, friendly, and likable.

In updates of the Gronlund and Anderson (1957) study, researchers (Carlson et al., 1984; Coie, Dodge, & Coppotelli, 1982) have examined the ways in which elementary schoolchildren view classmates who fit the extreme types of social status. Coie, Dodge, and Coppotelli (1982) assessed these peer perceptions in terms of six specific aspects of social behavior: cooperates, leads, acts shy, disrupts, fights, and seeks help. Findings indicated that rejected children scored high on disrupts, fights, and seeks help, while popular children scored high on cooperation and leadership. Neglected children received high ratings only for the category of acts shy. Following these earlier results, Carlson, Lahey, and Neeper (1984) also found that rejected elementary schoolchildren were perceived by their peers to behave in a distinctly more negative manner than either neglected or accepted children. Carlson et al. (1984) did not, however, find significant differences in peer assessments of neglected versus accepted children. The behavior patterns of these groups were both described in predominantly prosocial terms.

Taken together, the results of these studies provide evidence that the two types of low-status children are indeed perceived differently by their classmates. Peers perceive rejected children as being antagonistic and aggressive. Neglected children apparently do not have quite as distinct a reputation among peers, but, if anything, tend to be perceived as quiet and shy. The results of two additional studies (Fench & Waas, 1985; Green et al., 1981) suggest that similar views are also held by the children's classroom teachers.

Green, Vosk, Forehand, and Beck (1981) compared groups of rejected, neglected, and accepted third graders on teacher ratings of school behavior. Although differences between neglected children and the other two groups were not clear-cut, rejected children received significantly higher ratings than accepted children on two dimensions of behavior. Rejected children scored higher on overall hyperactivity, which included the specific items of restless, excitable, disturbs, and demands teacher attention. They also scored higher on inattentive-passive, which assessed their lack of concentration and tendency to daydream.

These results were paralleled in more recent research by French and Waas (1985). In the study, teachers rated socially rejected second- and fifth-grade children as having widespread behavior problems. The set of problems attributed to rejected children included aggression, hostile isolation, task avoidance, and manifest anxiety. Not surprisingly, the teachers' reports were less revealing with regard to the behavioral profiles of neglected children. Neglected children were reported to have significantly more overall school behavior problems than popular children, but were not described as exhibiting any of the overt kinds of problems that were attributed to rejected children. This pattern of findings thus fits with those obtained from the other studies of peer and teacher perceptions. Among their classmates and teachers, rejected children tend to come across as hostile and disruptive. Neglected children, by contrast, tend to leave little clear-cut impression at all.

Direct Observations of Low-status Children

Peer and teacher assessments have provided valuable insights into the classroom reputation of rejected and neglected children. But, from what specific behavior patterns do the children's reputations stem? Furthermore, do the reputations even reflect an accurate image of the children's actual interaction styles? It is by addressing questions like these that direct observational methods have made an integral contribution to research on the behavioral correlates of children's peer status.

Coie, Dodge, and their colleagues (Coie & Kupersmidt, 1983; Dodge, 1983; Dodge, Coie & Brakke, 1982) have conducted an active program of research based on direct observations of children in both naturalistic and analogue settings. Their work has focused on the precise delineation of the types of status that children may hold within their peer groups (e.g., rejected versus neglected). It has also been characterized by a focus on relatively specific patterns of social behavior. The findings that have been reported to date document the utility of the approach.

In the first of the studies, Dodge, Coie, and Brakke (1982) examined children's interactions across two separate aspects of the school environment: in the classroom during independent work period, and on the playground during recess. Subjects included third- and fifth-grade children who were classified into rejected, neglected, popular, and average status groups.

Analysis of the observational data indicated that the rejected children exhibited significantly more aggression than any of the other children. This was coupled with a tendency to engage in context-inappropriate behavior. For example, the rejected children were frequently off task during the classroom work period, daydreaming, wandering, or attempting to initiate contact with peers. They, in fact, made comparatively more social approaches during the classroom work period than did any of the other children under study. Given such disruptive behavior, it is not surprising that the rejected children were rebuffed by peers significantly more often than were popular or average children. Nor is it surprising that they spent significantly more time interacting with teachers (e.g., receiving directions, being reprimanded, or asking for help).

Dodge, Coie, and Brakke (1982) also attempted to characterize the behavior patterns of neglected children. The profile that emerged from their results was one of low social visibility. Of all the children under study, the neglected children remained on task the most and approached peers the least during the independent work period. Their apparent reluctance to initiate peer interaction also carried over into recess, even though this was the time when interaction among most class members was at its highest. When the neglected children did initiate contact with peers, they were more likely to be rebuffed than were either popular or average children. This proved to be one of the only points of similarity between the neglected and rejected groups.

Based on their findings, Dodge, Coie, and Brakke (1982) speculated that peer-directed aggression and deviant social approach patterns may be important variables in the explanation of rejected and neglected status. Rejected children acted aggressively toward their peers. Furthermore, when they made prosocial approaches, their timing was poor and they came across as being disruptive. Neglected children, on the other hand, were neither aggressive nor disruptive. Instead, they made too few social approaches to be able to integrate successfully into ongoing peer interactions.

The investigators (Dodge, Coie, & Brakke, 1982) warned that support for these speculations came from observations of children who had already acquired their status as rejected or neglected. As others (e.g., Moore, 1967; Renshaw & Asher, 1982) have also advised, a fundamental question concerning causality therefore remained. Did the observed behaviors cause the children's low social status, or were the behaviors a consequence of low social status?

The question of causality provided the impetus for two subsequent studies (Coie & Kupersmidt, 1983; Dodge, 1983). Dodge (1983) responded by designing a short-term longitudinal study to examine the development of social status over time. Six playgroups were formed for the study. Each group was made up of eight 7-year-old boys who had been previously unacquainted with one another. The groups met for eight play sessions, during which time the children's interactions were observed. Sociometric information was then obtained at the end of the last play session.

Dodge found that the boys' behaviors significantly predicted the social status that they came to acquire. Boys who became rejected directed significantly more verbal abuse and physical aggression toward their peers than did boys of average status. This pattern of aggressive behavior began with the first play session. In contrast, boys who became neglected refrained from aggressive behavior, and engaged in significantly more solitary play than boys of average status. The neglected boys also made fewer social approaches than average, but this tendency did not appear until the later play sessions.

Results of the Dodge (1983) study support a mixed set of conclusions with regard to the question of causality. A pattern of peer-directed aggression was implicated as a possible cause of rejected status. Boys who became rejected behaved antisocially beginning with their first encounter in the new peer group. On the other hand, a pattern of infrequent social approach behavior appeared to result more as a consequence of low social status. Boys who became neglected socially approached peers with a high frequency during early play sessions. The low rates of social approach behavior which have been previously observed among neglected children (Dodge, Coie, & Brakke, 1982) did not emerge until later sessions. By that time, status distinctions within the groups had become clearly established.

Like Dodge (1983), Coie and Kupersmidt (1983) observed the behaviors of children who had been placed in groups of previously unfamiliar peers. They compared these behaviors with the behaviors of children interacting in groups of familiar peers. The purpose was to identify patterns of behavior that are related to the emergence versus the maintenance of low social status.

Coie and Kupersmidt created 10 playgroups of fourth-grade boys on the basis of the boys' classroom social status. They placed four boys in each group. Of the four, one was a rejected child, one was neglected, one was popular, and one was average in status. Five of the groups were composed of boys who came from different schools and who thus did not know one another (unfamiliar groups). In each of the other five groups, the boys came from the same classroom and were all familiar with one another (familiar groups). The groups met once a week for 6 weeks.

Coie and Kupersmidt found that the boys' classroom status scores were significantly related to their final play group status scores. Classroom status positions thus tended to be re-established in the new social situations. Rejected boys conformed most fully to their stereotypical social patterns. They were highly interactive and talkative whether they were playing with familiar or unfamiliar peers. Furthermore, they exhibited significantly more antisocial behavior than any other boys. This latter finding reinforces earlier speculations (Dodge, 1983; Dodge, Coie, & Brakke, 1982) that a pattern of peer-directed aggression may contribute to both the emergence and the maintenance of rejected status.

Whereas the behavior of rejected boys was similar across familiar and unfamiliar groups, neglected boys displayed somewhat different patterns of behavior among familiar versus unfamiliar peers. Among familiar peers, neglected boys were the least interactive of all the status types. Among unfamiliar peers, however, the neglected boys broke away from their usual social patterns to become more active and outgoing. The presence of familiar peers thus seemed to have constrained the neglected boys, and compelled them to maintain their low-visibility role. This finding fits with Dodge's (1983) speculation that neglected children may develop their characteristic pattern of infrequent social approach behavior as a response to negative experiences with peers.

Overall, the findings from these recent studies on the behavioral correlates of children's peer relationship problems demonstrate important differences that exist between rejected and neglected children. The two types of low-status children have been found to exhibit distinct behavioral styles which are reflected in distinctly different classroom reputations. Rejected children tend to irritate and to strike out against their peers. Neglected children tend to maintain a low-key social profile, acting in ways that minimize the attention they receive. Although distinct, each of these patterns clearly limits the children's integration into the peer social system.

As efforts to understand children's peer relationship problems continue, we will need to learn more about the behaviors that relate to rejected and neglected status in girls. Several of the major studies in this area (Coie & Kupersmidt, 1983; Dodge, 1983) have been limited to all-male samples. Given that a number of the behavioral patterns identified in those studies are more characteristic of boys in general (e.g., direct aggression) (Maccoby & Jacklin 1974), it is not clear whether the findings may be applied to the experiences of low-status girls. The results of a recent study by Ladd (1983) are suggestive in this regard, however. Ladd discovered that even when low-status boys and girls do not differ in the content of their behavior, they may nevertheless differ in style. Whereas rejected boys may be physically aggressive, for instance, rejected girls may be argumentative and verbally aggressive. It thus seems likely that the exploration of sex-related differences will be a productive direction for future sociometric research.

Along with gender differences, it will also be important to examine developmental differences in the patterns that characterize children's peer status. The distinction between rejected and neglected status has extended our understanding of social adjustment problems in school-age children, but has rarely been applied in research with preschool samples (see Goldman,

Corsini, & deUrioste, 1980; Peery, 1979). It remains to be seen, therefore, whether the rejected–neglected scheme is useful for classifying the types of difficulties that young children experience in peer group relations.

A more basic question left unresolved by current research is whether rejected and neglected children are both at risk in terms of their interpersonal adjustment. Rejected children exhibit obvious social problems which are likely to continue throughout later years (e.g., Coie & Dodge, 1983). The problems of neglected children would seem to be less significant, although a clear picture of what these children are like cannot be drawn from the existing data base. The "quietness" of some neglected children may reflect an inability to interact effectively with peers. Other neglected childen may keep a low social profile simply because they prefer to focus on individual rather than group pursuits. As Asher (1983) has noted, an intensive study of neglected children is needed to gain a more detailed account of the group's characteristics.

Finally, we need to learn more about how children's classroom reputations are acquired and maintained. As low-status children are labeled by peers, it may become increasingly difficult for the children to overcome their social problems (e.g., Dodge & Frame, 1982). What types of information do children use in attaching labels to one another? From what sources is this information obtained — teachers, friends, the children's own observations? These questions would provide an intriguing basis for future research. The issue of how teachers influence children's judgments of one another may be particularly important to pursue (Cairns, 1983). Research reviewed earlier indicates that peer and teacher perceptions of low-status children do have a strong basis in reality. Still, the possibility exists that teachers somehow mediate children's reputations among peers, and thus influence the children's peer status. Evidence supporting this notion has been obtained in studies with high school (Flanders & Havumaki, 1960) and mildly retarded elementary school students (Morrison, Forness, & MacMillan, 1983). Similar work should now be conducted with more general samples of preschool and school-age children.

THE CHILD'S PERSPECTIVE ON PEER RELATIONSHIP PROBLEMS

Up to this point, the review has revealed a growing diversification in how researchers view children's peer relationship problems. This diversification has not been limited, however, to a concern for sorting out the separate behavioral problems that are experienced by rejected versus neglected children. In a parallel and, in many ways, more striking development, researchers have also recently expanded the study of children's peer relationship problems to include greater consideration of children's perspectives on their own social situations.

Theoretically, the emerging interest in the child's perspective has been inspired by the cognitive-behavioral model of adjustment disorders (Meichenbaum, Bream, & Cohen, in press). The basic premise of this model is that cognitive and affective processes play a major role in determining the presence, or absence, of serious adjustment problems. Stress is not assumed to derive from any given situation or outcome per se (e.g., social rejection). Instead, it is assumed to be a function of how the individual appraises the outcome. With regard to children's peer relationship problems, then, the cognitive-behavioral model implies that the child's appraisal of his or her own social situation is of paramount concern. In order to understand fully the problems that children are experiencing in peer relations, researchers must look beyond objective aspects of the children's social situations (e.g., peer status, behavioral patterns) to consider the perceptions and feelings of the children themselves (see Asher, Hymel, & Renshaw, 1984; Hymel, 1983b).

In applying these assumptions on the empirical level, investigators have begun by asking whether there is in fact any direct connection between children's peer status and their subjective sense of well-being. Recent studies have been designed to examine the link between peer status and various aspects of children's self-evaluations (e.g., Hymel, 1983b; Wheeler & Ladd, 1982). Other recent studies have been conducted to compare the general affective states of low- versus high-status children (e.g., Asher, Hymel, & Renshaw, 1984; Jacobsen, Lahey, & Strauss, 1983). The results of these studies are reviewed next, along with data from relevant prior investigations.

In the studies under review, researchers have assessed social status in a variety of different ways. Only a limited number of studies (Asher & Wheeler, 1983; Dahlquist & Ottinger, 1983; Waas & French, 1984) have incorporated a distinction between rejected and neglected children. Cognitive and affective profiles of specific status types cannot therefore be presented to parallel the behavioral profiles that were presented earlier. Instead, the contribution of these studies comes in documenting the importance of the child's perspective, thereby establishing a new direction for research on children's peer relationship problems.

Peer Status and Children's Self-evaluations

Self-perception of social status. When considering the child's perspective, it is important to know whether children are even aware of their own status among peers. Several studies have been designed to address this question. One group of investigators have focused on children's awareness of their specific status within the classroom peer group (Ausubel, Schiff, & Gasser, 1952; Hymel, 1983b; Krantz & Burton, 1986). The central issue here has been the correspondence between the sociometric ratings that children *actually* received from their classmates and the ratings that the children *expected* to receive. Other researchers have focused on children's self-perceptions of their general effectiveness in establishing relationships with peers (Bukowski & Newcomb, 1983; Garrison, Earls, & Kindlon, 1983; Hymel, 1983b; Kurdek & Krile, 1982). These latter researchers have drawn upon the work of Harter (1982; Harter & Pike, 1984) who has developed instruments to assess children's self-judgments within various life domains, including the domain of peer acceptance. The items on Harter's self-perceived peer acceptance scales refer to such issues as being easy to like, having a lot of friends, and doing things with other kids.

In studies with older elementary schoolchildren, positive correlations have consistently been obtained between sociometric status and both expected sociometric ratings and self-perceptions of general social effectiveness (Ausubel et al., 1952; Bukowski & Newcomb, 1983; Hymel, 1983b; Kurdek & Krile, 1982). These results suggest that children of age 8 and older tend to have at least some awareness of how well they are functioning in the peer social system. Children who are accepted by their classmates tend to perceive themselves as successful in peer relations; children who are not accepted by their classmates tend to lack a sense of social success. At the same time, the moderate magnitude of obtained correlations suggests that there may also be considerable variability within status levels. Evidently not *all* high-status elementary schoolchildren feel that they have been successful in establishing peer relationships, while not all low-status children consider themselves to have been socially unsuccessful.

Findings in contrast to these have emerged from research with children below the age of 8. For this age group, which includes children in preschool through second grade, only negligible correlations have been found between measures of children's self-perceived and their actual peer relations (Garrison, Earls, & Kindlon, 1983; Harter & Pike, 1984; Krantz & Burton, 1986). There thus appear to be interesting developmental differences in the extent to which children's social self-perceptions can be expected to be realistic. Prior to the third grade, distortions in such self-judgments may be the norm. As Harter (1983; Harter & Pike, 1984) has pointed out, the young child's egocentrism may allow the wish to be socially successful to intrude upon the child's judgment of his or her real self. This contention is supported by findings that young children do, in fact, tend to report somewhat inflated ratings of their own social status (Harter & Pike, 1984).

Self-perceptions of social abilities. Efforts to explicate the child's perspective on peer relationship problems have also included assessments of children's perceptions about their own social abilities. Confidence in one's abilities to achieve interpersonal goals is assumed to be an important component of social adjustment (Asher, 1983; Goetz & Dweck, 1980). Researchers have, therefore, begun to look for a link between the amount of confidence children have in their own social abilities and the problems the children encounter in peer relations. Studies conducted to date have been primarily limited to analyses of the direct relationship between peer status and children's perceptions about their own social abilities.

The most specific information available has come from recent work by Wheeler and Ladd (1982). The focus of this work was the development of the Children's Self-Efficacy for Peer Interaction Scale, designed to measure elementary schoolchildren's confidence in their own social persuasion abilities. In administering the scale to samples of third- through fifth-grade children, Wheeler and Ladd obtained relatively low, but significant, correlations between social self-efficacy and sociometric status. Low-status children expressed significantly less confidence in their own social persuasion abilities than did their higher-status peers.

Additional information about children's social self-confidence has come from studies of the causal attributions that children make for their own interpersonal successes and failures (Ames, Ames, & Garrison, 1977; Dahlquist & Ottinger, 1983; Goetz & Dweck, 1980; Hymel, Freigang, Franke, Both, Bream, & Borys, 1983; Waas and French, 1984). In these studies, children have typically been asked to explain why given hypothetical social situations would have occurred (e.g., "The girls in your class had a party but did not invite you. Why do you think that would happen?"). Their responses have been characterized in terms of broad dimensions of causality, and then examined in relation to the children's sociometric status. Taken together, the results have provided fairly consistent support for a relationship between peer status and children's tendency to make internal versus external attributions for hypothetical social outcomes.

Dahlquist and Ottinger (1983) found, for example, that while popular children tended to attribute social outcomes to internal causes, both rejected and neglected children tended to attribute such outcomes to external causes. These results were replicated by Waas and French (1984). Data from still other studies have documented even more specific differences in how children of each status type explain their social experiences (Ames, Ames, & Garrison, 1977; Goetz & Dweck, 1980; Hymel et al., 1983). In these investigations, low-status children have been found to accept the blame for failure in hypothetical social situations, but to disavow personal credit for success. The reverse pattern has been found among more popular children.

The overall implication that can be drawn from the results of the attribution studies is that low-status children tend to have less confidence in their own social abilities than do popular children. They tend to see themselves as lacking control over peer interactions, in general, and are particularly prone to dismiss the possibility that their own actions could be instrumental in eliciting positive responses from peers. These conclusions are also consistent with the results of Wheeler and Ladd's (1982) work on social self-efficacy. Despite such cross-study consistencies, however, the conclusions must nevertheless be stated with caution. The magnitude of relationships between sociometric status and children's perceptions about their own social abilities has been low, so exceptions to the general pattern can be expected to occur. This point is important in that it corroborates what was learned from the recent studies on children's perceptions of their own peer status. One might predict that popular children would invariably enjoy more positive self-evaluations than less popular children. Yet, as Hartup (1983) previously concluded, the relation between self-attitudes and social acceptance appears to be somewhat more complicated than this.

Peer Status and Children's Affective States

An 8-year-old boy said to be depressed over accusations that he stole $4 at school was found hanged by his own belt. The boy's father told news reporters that his son had been depressed after classmates accused him of stealing $4 from their teacher's purse. The child had said that he didn't steal the money, but that he wasn't going back to school because the other kids kept picking on him ("Boy Found . . . ", 1984).

The study of the affective experience associated with children's peer relationship problems represents a virtually unexplored research direction (see Sroufe, Schork, Motti, Lawroski, & LaFreniere, 1984). Yet, as the above news story so graphically illustrates, the study of emotions should prove to be extremely informative. In the few investigations that have been conducted, researchers have examined the link between peer status and the three affective variables of anxiety, depression, and loneliness. The results of these investigations are reviewed next.

Anxiety. Preliminary descriptions of the affective correlates of peer relationship problems have come from studies of the relation between sociometric status and anxiety. In initial studies of this kind, researchers discovered that low-status children tend to experience greater feelings of general anxiety than do their higher-status peers (see Hartup, 1970, for a review). For instance, McCandless, Castaneda, and Palermo (1956) obtained a significant negative correlation between peer status and general anxiousness for a sample of fourth- through sixth-grade children. Cowen, Zax, Klein, Izzo, and Trost (1965) obtained similar results in working with a group of third graders. Such findings appear to be representative of those obtained in other comparable studies.

Beyond this early work on the link between peer status and children's general anxiety level, researchers have also taken beginning steps to explore the specific anxieties that children experience with regard to peer social relations. Buhrmester (1982) recently developed a self-report questionnaire which assesses elementary schoolchildren's anxieties about making and keeping friends (e.g., "How worried do you get about being liked by the kids at school?"). In a follow-up study using the questionnaire, he obtained a significant negative correlation between social anxiety and sociometric status. The children who were least accepted by their classmates tended to feel the most nervous and worried about their own peer relationships.

In sum, it appears that anxiety is in fact experienced to a greater degree by children of low as compared with high peer status. At the same time, it must be noted that even given a rather specific measure of social anxiety (Buhrmester, 1982), correlations between anxiety and sociometric status have remained in the low-to-moderate range. This fact deserves mention because it underscores the potential complexity of any relationship that exists between children's peer status and their individual affective states.

Depression is another likely component of the affective experience underlying children's peer relationship problems. In an exploratory study of children's overall patterns of emotional response, Harter and Simovich (reported in Harter, 1984) asked elementary schoolchildren to describe their emotional reactions to success and failure within the area of peer social relations. Depression was the children's predominant emotional reaction to failure in peer relations. Of all the children interviewed, 46% said that they would respond to serious peer relationship problems by feeling sad and depressed.

Given descriptive evidence such as this, researchers have not been surprised to find that depression is significantly related to children's status in the peer group. Three recent studies have been conducted to examine the relationship between sociometric status and depression (Jacobsen, Lahey, & Strauss, 1983; Lefkowitz & Tesiny, 1980; Vosk, Forehand, Parker, & Rickard, 1982), and the general findings have all been the same. Namely, low-status elementary schoolchildren have been found to be significantly more depressed than their higher-status classmates. It thus seems reasonable to assume that depression is an important dimension of children's social adjustment problems, one that should receive additional research attention.

Loneliness. The most specific information available with regard to the emotional implications of peer relationship problems has come from research on children's loneliness (Asher, Hymel, & Renshaw, 1984; Asher & Wheeler, 1983). Asher, Hymel, & Renshaw (1984) recently developed a self-report questionnaire to study loneliness and social dissatisfaction in elementary schoolchildren. Of particular interest have been differences in children's feelings of loneliness and social dissatisfaction as a function of the children's sociometric status.

The loneliness questionnaire has been administered to samples of third-through sixth-grade children who have been classified according to both sociometric ratings and positive sociometric nominations (Asher, Hymel, & Renshaw, 1984; Hymel, 1983b). As would be expected, the lower-status children have reported significantly greater loneliness and social dissatisfaction than their more accepted peers. What has been intriguing, however, is the variability that has occurred within status levels. Many of the low-status children have not expressed serious dissatisfaction with their own peer relationships. In contrast, a number of the popular children have described themselves as feeling left out and alone.

In a follow-up study, Asher and Wheeler (1983) subclassified low-status children into rejected and neglected groups. They found that rejected children were significantly more lonely than the children in all other status groups. Neglected children, on the other hand, were no more lonely than children of average sociometric status, and only somewhat more lonely than popular children. These are striking results given the traditional assumption that *all* low-status children are at risk in terms of their social adjustment. Above all, the data provide added evidence of the need to distinguish between rejected and neglected children. Both groups of children lack widespread peer acceptance, yet, for some reason, only rejected children tend to express a strong subjective sense of social isolation.

Taken as a whole, the results reviewed in this section demonstrate that children's social status among peers is generally predictive of the children's subjective sense of well-being. Children of low peer status tend to experience a more negative set of self-perceptions than do children of higher peer status, judging themselves to be relatively incompetent and unsuccessful when it comes to social relationships. Low-status children likewise tend to experience more emotional problems than their higher status peers. In research conducted to date, low sociometric status has been found to be associated with a number of negative affective states, including anxiety, depression, and loneliness.

Still, it must be emphasized that these represent only general trends. Obtained correlations between peer status and indicators of children's subjective sense of well-being, although significant, have been rather low, and specific exceptions to the general patterns have been observed. It is precisely these exceptions, however — the low-status children who are contented and the popular children who are not — that document the importance of considering the child's perspective on peer relationship problems. It is true that researchers have made only preliminary efforts to explore the thoughts and feelings that children experience with regard to their own peer relations. Yet, in so doing, they have offered what Meichenbaum et al. (in press, p. 21) refer to as a "promising agenda" for future peer relations research.

As the content of this research agenda takes shape, several issues should be given high-priority attention. First, studies are needed to examine the subjective outlooks of rejected versus neglected children. Clearly, children with such different visible social profiles would also be expected to possess differing subjective perspectives on themselves and their own social situations. Consider the evidence provided by Asher and Wheeler (1983). They discovered that whereas rejected children are much more lonely than the rest of their peers, neglected children are only somewhat more lonely than average or popular children. A conclusion that has since been drawn from the findings is that rejected children are generally a more at-risk social status group than neglected children. Such a conclusion obviously addresses an issue of important practical concern. Nevertheless, it will remain tentative until further information is available to describe the incidence of psychological adjustment problems (e.g., low self-esteem, depression) in rejected versus neglected children.

Findings to date also leave open important questions concerning the role that children's self-perceptions and emotional states play in *contributing* to the children's social problems. It is probable that a poor self-image and feelings of emotional distress represent a cause as well as a consequence of problematic peer relations. There is evidence, for example, that children who lack confidence in their own social abilities tend to exhibit little persistence or flexibility in their attempts to achieve social goals (Goetz & Dweck, 1980; Krasnor, 1983). It has similarly been demonstrated that the frequent display of negative affect can interfere with a child's effectiveness among peers, no matter how socially skillful the child might be (Sroufe et al., 1984). By examining the implications that self-perceptions and emotions have for children's overt interaction patterns, we may gain key insights into the processes through which children's peer problems are created and maintained.

A final issue left to be resolved is why obtained correlations between peer status and indicators of children's subjective sense of well-being have not been stronger. The overall magnitude of relationships in this area of research has been relatively low, certainly lower than would be expected given traditional assumptions regarding the significance of childhood peer relations (see Hartup, 1983).

In order to explicate the link between peer status and children's sense of well-being, it may be necessary to consider the influence of intervening social-cognitive factors. Peplau and her associates (e.g., Peplau, Miceli, & Morasch, 1982) have argued that a useful direction would be to consider the personal standards, or aspirations, that children have for their own peer relations. According to this point of view, researchers should shift their emphasis from the objective level of children's peer relationships, and consider instead the extent to which such relationships meet the children's desired patterns, or aspirations, for peer relations. A low-status child who has correspondingly low social aspirations may actually feel quite comfortable with his or her personal circumstances. In contrast, a child who is popular by external standards may nevertheless have difficulty maintaining a subjective sense of satisfaction and security if he or she is driven by unrealistically high social aspirations. These arguments are appealing. Yet, it remains for researchers to evaluate their validity.

SOCIAL INTERVENTION TECHNIQUES

Even without formal assessments such as sociometric tests or behavioral observations, parents and teachers usually notice, and become concerned, when children lack friends in school. Once sparked, their concern generally turns to the question of why the children are encountering difficulties in peer interactions. Underlying this search for an explanation is a wish to obtain clues as to how they can best help the children overcome their social problems. The research literature on social intervention techniques is expanding steadily. Although more work is needed, a number of techniques have been found to be effective in remedying children's peer relationship problems. Furthermore, these techniques appear to be ones that could be employed successfully by practitioners in a wide variety of settings. Tyne and Flynn (1979) have shown, for example, that classroom teachers can improve the peer status of disliked students if simply provided with suggestions about possible intervention techniques!

As mentioned, a key to successful intervention is the ability to match the nature of the intervention to the specific needs of the children involved. Perhaps the most obvious need of many low-status children is the need to learn new skills for interacting with peers. Research reviewed earlier (e.g., Dodge, Coie, & Brakke, 1982) indicated that both rejected and neglected children tend to behave in ways that limit their acceptance among peers. Results from additional studies (e.g., Richard & Dodge, 1982) suggest that these maladaptive behavior patterns may stem from a lack of knowledge about effective interaction strategies. In these studies, children have been presented with hypothetical social problems (e.g., "What if you wanted to make friends with a new kid in the neighborhood?"), and asked to give their ideas about how to solve the problems. Low-status children have typically been able to generate fewer alternative solutions than their higher status peers. Their ideas for dealing with social problems have likewise tended to be either too vague to be effective, or unnecessarily negative in tone (Renshaw & Asher, 1982).

Based on the evidence that low-status children often lack knowledge of how to behave socially, researchers have attempted to improve the children's peer relations through direct instruction in social skills (Gottman, Gonso, & Schuler, 1976; Gresham & Nagle, 1980; Hymel & Asher, 1977; Ladd, 1981; LaGreca & Santogrossi, 1980; Oden & Asher, 1977). The basic instructional plan followed in these social skill training studies has been threefold. First, low-status children have been given verbal instruction on ways to make their peer interactions more mutually satisfying and productive. For example, they have been taught general guidelines for being cooperative and supportive (e.g., Oden & Asher, 1977), as well as more specific techniques for engaging peers in play (e.g., LaGreca & Santogrossi, 1980). Following such instruction, the children have been given opportunities to practice the trained skills in either role play or actual peer group situations. Finally, the children have been encouraged to reflect on their performance in the practice sessions, and to consider how their newfound skills could be used in day-to-day social interactions.

Taken together, the results of the social skill training studies are quite encouraging. With only two exceptions (Hymel & Asher, 1977; LaGreca & Santogrossi, 1980), the studies have revealed that direct instruction in social skills is effective in increasing low-status children's acceptance among peers. More importantly, the beneficial effect of skill training has been shown to be a lasting one, with trained children's level of peer acceptance continuing to improve as much as a year following intervention (Oden & Asher, 1977). The message here is thus a clear one. Children can improve their social functioning if given support and guidance from adults. In many cases, the most appropriate form of guidance is direct coaching in social interaction concepts.

While coaching programs may remedy deficits in children's social knowledge, there are nevertheless other important reasons why low-status children display maladaptive social behaviors (Renshaw & Asher, 1982). Consider the case of the rejected child. Researchers have reported that rejected children frequently behave in a disruptive manner during classroom work periods, and that this behavior pattern contributes to the children's peer relationship problems (Dodge, Coie, & Brakke, 1982). It is of course possible that rejected children behave disruptively because they do not understand the rules of classroom social conduct. Yet, it is also plausible that the children behave disruptively because they are unable to occupy themselves with the assigned academic tasks. This latter explanation fits with what is known about the academic achievement of low-status children. Data are available to indicate that rejected children do, in fact, tend to experience rather substantial academic problems. Comparable academic problems have not been noted among neglected children as a group (e.g., Green, Forehand, Beck, & Vosk, 1980; Green et al., 1981).

Recently, an intervention study was conducted to examine the connection between rejected children's academic and social problems (Coie & Krehbiel, 1984). The investigators provided intensive academic tutoring for fourth-grade students who were both rejected by peers and deficient in basic academic skills. Matched controls received either social skill training or no intervention at all. As predicted, the academic tutoring led to significant improvements in the rejected children's social status. Surprisingly, though, the social status gains produced by the academic tutoring were even stronger than those produced by the social skill training. By overcoming their academic deficits, the tutored children were apparently able to increase their on-task work behavior and conduct themselves in a manner that was more acceptable to classmates. They were likewise able to elicit more positive attention from teachers, which undoubtedly helped to enhance their reputations among peers further. Above all, these findings represent a call for diversity in how adults treat children's peer relationship problems. When such problems occur along with serious academic problems, intensive academic intervention may be necessary if the children are to become fully functioning, and accepted, members of their classroom groups.

The aim of the intervention techniques described thus far has been to increase low-status children's peer acceptance by bringing about improvements in the children's classroom behavior. Yet, is it reasonable to assume that peer atttitudes toward the low-status children will necessarily improve as the children's behavior improves (see Asher, 1983)? Based on research evidence (e.g., Coie, Dodge, & Coppotelli, 1982) we know that peers tend to maintain rather negative perceptions of both rejected and neglected children. It may be difficult for the low-status children to modify these negative reputations even given the benefits of an effective social skill or academic training program (Putallaz, 1982).

In line with these concerns, Bierman (1983; Bierman & Furman, 1984) has argued that behavioral change may be necessary but not sufficient for fostering peer acceptance of low-status children. Her work documents the importance of combining skill training with structured opportunities for trained children to make their new competencies known to peers. Teachers and other practitioners could accomplish this in a number of ways. As has been done in successful social skill training studies (e.g., Oden & Asher, 1977), behavioral change activities could be coupled with peer pairing. The basic plan, here, is to give low-status children a chance to practice the new skills they are learning with higher status peer partners. Once these peer partners recognize that the low-status children can be rewarding play- or workmates, their acceptance will hopefully assist the low-status children in gaining entry to a broader segment of the classroom peer group (Bierman & Furman, 1984).

A related technique for helping low-status children overcome reputational problems involves the use of cooperative group projects. Under this scheme, low-status children who are being trained in new skills are also placed into small work groups with more popular classmates. The groups are then assigned interesting tasks (e.g., staging a play) which can only be accomplished if all group members work together. By imposing a cooperative goal, the group projects give the more popular children a reason to interact with low-status peers whom they previously would have avoided out of habit. In the process, the popular children often discover new bases for liking the low-status children, and hence become more willing to integrate them into other peer group activities (e.g., Bierman & Furman, 1984; Johnson & Johnson, 1983).

It is certainly true that low-status children who lack friends exhibit the most salient social problems. Recent work on children's social self-perceptions has revealed, however, that low peer status may not be the only appropriate indicator of the need for intervention (Blyth, 1983; Dweck, 1981). Indeed, some low-status children apparently remain contented without becoming part of the classroom social circle. Some popular children, by contrast, appear from all outward signs to "have it made" socially, but themselves feel very troubled and alone (e.g., Asher, Hymel, & Renshaw, 1984). This potential variability requires that adults interested in children's social problems stay closely attuned to the subjective outlook of each individual child.

The focus on children's social self-perceptions is so new that specific interventions aimed at enhancing such self-perceptions have not yet been developed and tested (Meichenbaum et al., in press). Even without empirical documentation, though, there are several general strategies that would seem to be useful in helping children maintain a healthy outlook on their own social lives. First, it seems important for parents and teachers to give children explicit opportunities to share any peer-related concerns they might have. Teachers could do this, for example, by giving older children the opportunity to write about social topics. The children could write about how they feel when a friend gets mad, or they could describe their probable reactions to being excluded from classmates' social activities. Puppets could be used to encourage younger children to express their thoughts and feelings about peer-related problems. In any case, experience indicates that children will often solicit advice on underlying social concerns once interest is expressed by a trusted adult.

In the same way, it seems important for adults to monitor carefully the kinds of social expectations they communicate to children. Several authors (Riesman, Glazer, & Denney, 1953; Rubin, 1980) have argued that adults in our culture tend to transmit the attitude that children should be liked by "all of the people all of the time." Such an unrealistic expectation, however, may leave many children feeling inadequate and insecure even after they attain relatively high levels of peer popularity. The appropriate goal for adults in fostering children's peer relations, then, is to create options without creating pressures. Children with an overly intense desire for peer approval may need special reinforcement whenever they take action *independent* of peers. For these children, the most comforting form of adult support could be permission *not* to try to "please all of the people all of the time."

CONCLUSION

Recent sociometric research has been characterized by an increasing diversification in how investigators view children's peer relationship problems. Progress has been made in sorting out the separate problems that are experienced by rejected versus neglected children. Children's self-perceptions and affective states have likewise been introduced as important sources for gaining insight into children's social adjustment problems. With these advances in descriptive knowledge has come new potential for developing effective social intervention programs. Thus, even though the focus of the chapter is on problems, the underlying theme is nevertheless quite positive.

Parents and teachers should follow the lead of researchers, and increase their own commitment to identifying and helping children who might be experiencing serious peer relationship problems. The same inquisitive attitude that has led to productive research in this area should also assist parents and teachers in accomplishing their more practical endeavors. By adopting a broad perspective and drawing information from a number of different sources, parents and teachers should be able to identify more clearly the social needs of individual children, and to create effective ways to meet those needs.

REFERENCES

Ames, R., Ames, C., & Garrison,, W. (1977). Children's causal ascriptions for positive and negative interpersonal outcomes. *Psychological Reports, 41,* 595–602.

Asher, S.R. (1983). Social competence and peer status: Recent advances and future directions. *Child Development, 54,* 1427–1434.

Asher, S.R., & Hymel, S. (1981). Children's social competence in peer relations: Sociometric and behavioral assessment. In J.D. Wine & M. Smye (Eds.), *Social competence* (pp. 125–157). New York: Guilford Press.

Asher, S.R., Hymel, S., & Renshaw, P.D. (1984). Loneliness in children. *Child Development, 55,* 1456–1464.

Asher, S.R., Oden, S.L., & Gottman, J.M. (1977). Children's friendships in school settings. In L.G. Katz (Ed.), *Current topics in early childhood education* (Vol. 1, pp. 33–61). Norwood, NJ: Ablex.

Asher, S.R., & Renshaw, P.D. (1981). Children without friends: Social knowledge and social-skill training. In S.R. Asher & J.M. Gottman (Eds.), *The development of children's friendships* (p. 273–296). New York: Cambridge University Press.

Asher, S.R., Renshaw, P.D., & Hymel, S. (1982). Peer relations and the development of social skills. In S.G. Moore & C.R. Cooper (Eds.), *The young child: Reviews of research* (Vol. 3, pp. 137–158). Washington, DC: National Association for the Education of Young Children.

Asher, S.R., & Wheeler, V.A. (1983, August). *Children's loneliness: A comparison of rejected and neglected peer status.* Paper presented at the annual meeting of the American Psychological Association, Anaheim, CA.

Ausubel, D.P., Schiff, H.M., & Gasser, E.B. (1952). A preliminary study of developmental trends in socioempathy: Accuracy of perception of own and others' sociometric status. *Child Development, 23,* 111–128.

Bierman, K.L. (1983, April). *The effects of social skills training on the interactions of unpopular and popular peers engaged in cooperative tasks.* Paper presented at the biennial meeting of the Society for Research in Child Development, Detroit.

Bierman, K.L., & Furman, W. (1984). The effects of social skills training and peer involvement on the social adjustment of preadolescents. *Child Development, 55,* 151–162.

Blyth, D.A. (1983). Surviving and thriving in the social world: A commentary on six new studies of popular, rejected, and neglected children. *Merrill–Palmer Quarterly, 29,* 449–458.

Boy found hanging. (1984, November). *Tallahassee Democrat,* p. 3B.

Bronfenbrenner, U. (1944). A constant frame of reference of sociometric research: Part II. Experiment and inference. *Sociometry, 7,* 40–75.

Buhrmester, D. (1982). *Children's concerns inventory manual.* (Available from Department of Psychology, University of Denver, Denver, CO 80208).

Bukowski, W.M., & Newcomb, A.F. (1983). The association between peer experiences and identity formation in early adolescence. *Journal of Early Adolescence, 3,* 265–274.

Cairns, R.B. (1983). Sociometry, psychometry, and social structure: A commentary on six recent studies of popular, rejected, and neglected children. *Merrill–Palmer Quarterly, 29,* 429–438.

Carlson, C.L., Lahey, B.B., & Neeper, R. (1984). Peer assessment of the social behavior of accepted, rejected, and neglected children. *Journal of Abnormal Child Psychology, 12,* 189–198.

Coie, J.D., & Dodge, K.A. (1983). Continuities and change in children's social status: A five-year longitudinal study. *Merrill–Palmer Quarterly, 29,* 261–282.

Coie, J.D., Dodge, K.A., & Coppotelli, H. (1982). Dimensions and types of social status: A cross-age perspective. *Developmental Psychology, 18,* 557–570.

Coie, J.D., & Krehbiel, G. (1984). Effects of academic tutoring on the social status of low-achieving, socially rejected children. *Child Development, 55,* 1465–1478.

Coie, J.D., & Kupersmidt, J.B. (1983). A behavioral analysis of emerging social status in boys' groups. *Child Development, 54,* 1400–1416.

Combs, M.L., & Slaby, D.A. (1977). Social-skills training with children. In B.B. Lahey & A.E. Kazdin (Eds.), *Advances in clinical child psychology: Vol. 1* (pp. 161–201). New York: Plenum.

Cowen, E.L., Pederson, A., Babigian, H., Izzo, L.D., & Trost, M.A. (1973). Long-term follow-up of early detected vulnerable children. *Journal of Consulting and Clinical Psychology, 41,* 438–446.

Cowen, E.L., Zax, M., Klein, R., Izzo, L.D., & Trost, M.A. (1965). The relation of anxiety in school children to school record, achievement, and behavioral measures. *Child Development, 36,* 685–695.

Dahlquist, L.M., & Ottinger, D.R. (1983). Locus of control and peer status: A scale for children's perceptions of social interactions. *Journal of Personality Assessment, 47,* 278–287.

Dodge, K. (1983). Behavioral antecedents of peer social status. *Child Development, 54,* 1386–1399.

Dodge, K., Coie, J., & Brakke, P. (1982). Behavior patterns of socially rejected and neglected preadolescents: The roles of social approach and aggression. *Journal of Abnormal Child Psychology, 10,* 389–410.

Dodge, K.A., & Frame, C.L. (1982). Social cognitive biases and deficits in aggressive boys. *Child Development, 53,* 620–635.

Dweck, C.S. (1981). Social-cognitive processes in children's friendships. In S.R. Asher & J.M. Gottman (Eds.), *The development of children's friendships* (pp. 322–333). New York: Cambridge University Press.

Flanders, N.A., & Havumaki, S. (1960). The effect of teacher-pupil contacts involving praise on the sociometric choices of students. *Journal of Educational Psychology, 51,* 65–68.

French, D.C., & Waas, G.A. (1985). Behavior problems of peer-neglected and peer-rejected elementary-age children: Parent and teacher perspectives. *Child Development, 56,* 246–252.

Garrison, W., Earls, F., & Kindlon, D. (1983). An application of the pictorial scale of perceived competence and acceptance within an epidemiological survey. *Journal of Abnormal Child Psychology, 11,* 367–377.

Goetz, T., & Dweck, C. (1980). Learned helplessness in social situations. *Journal of Personality and Social Psychology, 39,* 246–255.

Goldman, J.A., Corsini, D.A., & deUrioste, R. (1980). Implications of positive and negative sociometric status for assessing the social competence of young children. *Journal of Applied Developmental Psychology, 1,* 209–220.

Gottman, J. (1977). Toward a definition of social isolation in children. *Child Development, 48,* 513–517.

Gottman, J., Gonso, J., & Schuler, P. (1976). Teaching social skills to isolated children. *Journal of Abnormal Child Psychology, 4,* 179–197.

Green, K.D., Forehand, R., Beck, S.J., & Vosk, B. (1980). An assessment of the relationship among measures of children's social competence and children's academic achievement. *Child Development, 51,* 1149–1156.

Green, K., Vosk, B., Forehand, R., & Beck, S. (1981). An examination of differences among sociometrically identified accepted, rejected, and neglected children. *Child Study Journal, 11*(3), 117–124.

Gresham, F.M., & Nagle, R.J. (1980). Social skills training with children: Responsiveness to modeling and coaching as a function of peer orientation. *Journal of Consulting and Clinical Psychology, 48,* 718–729.

Gronlund, N.E. (1959). *Sociometry in the classroom.* New York: Harper.

Gronlund, N., & Anderson, L. (1957). Personality characteristics of socially accepted, socially neglected, and socially rejected junior high school pupils. *Educational Administration and Supervision, 43,* 329–338.

Harter, S. (1982). The perceived competence scale for children. *Child Development, 53,* 87–97.

Harter, S. (1983). Developmental perspectives on the self-system. In E.M. Hetherington (Ed.), *Handbook of child psychology: Socialization, personality, and social development* (pp. 275–385). New York: Wiley.

Harter, S. (1984). Competence as a dimension of self-evaluation: Toward a comprehensive model of self-worth. In R. Leahy (Ed.), *The development of the self.* New York: Academic Press.

Harter, S., & Pike, R. (1984). The pictorial scale of perceived competence and social acceptance for young children. *Child Development, 55,* 1969–1982.

Hartup, W.W. (1970). Peer interaction and social organization. In P.H. Mussen (Ed.), *Carmichael's manual of child psychology* (Vol. 2, pp. 361–456). New York: Wiley.

Hartup, W.W. (1983). The peer system. In E.M. Hetherington (Ed.), *Handbook of child psychology: Vol. 4. Socialization, personality, and social development* (pp. 103–196). New York: Wiley.

Hartup, W.W., Glazer, J., & Charlesworth, R. (1967). Peer reinforcement and sociometric status. *Child Development, 38,* 1017–1024.

Hayvren, M., & Hymel, S. (1984). Ethical issues in sociometric testing: Impact of sociometric measures on interactive behavior. *Developmental Psychology, 20,* 844–849.

Hymel, S. (1983a). Preschool children's peer relations: Issues in sociometric assessment. *Merrill–Palmer Quarterly, 29,* 237–260.

Hymel, S. (1983b, April). *Social isolation and rejection in children: The child's perspective.* Paper presented at the biennial meeting of the Society for Research in Child Development, Detroit.

Hymel, S., & Asher, S.R. (1977). *Assessment and training of isolated children's social skills.* Paper presented at the biennial meeting of the Society for Research in Child Development, New Orleans. (ERIC Document Reproduction Service No. ED 136 930)

Hymel, S., Freigang, R., Franke, S., Both, L., Bream, L., & Borys, S. (1983, June). Children's attributions for social situations: Variations as a function of social status and self-perception variables. In *Children's attributions for social experience.* Symposium conducted at the annual meeting of the Canadian Psychological Association, Winnipeg.

Jacobsen, R.H., Lahey, B.B., & Strauss, C.C. (1983). Correlates of depressed mood in normal children. *Journal of Abnormal Child Psychology, 11,* 29–40.

Johnson, R.T., & Johnson, D.W. (1983). Effects of cooperative, competitive, and individualistic learning experiences on social development. *Exceptional Children, 49,* 323–329.

Krantz, M., & Burton, C.B. (1986). The development of the social cognition of social status. *Journal of Genetic Psychology, 147*(1), 89–95.

Krasnor, L.R. (1983, April). *Social attribution and social problem-solving.* Paper presented at the biennial meeting of the Society for Research in Child Development, Detroit.

Kurdek, L., & Krile, D. (1982). A developmental analysis of the relation between peer acceptance and both interpersonal understanding and perceived social self-competence. *Child Development, 53,* 1485–1491.

Ladd, G.W. (1981). Effectiveness of a social learning method for enhancing children's social interaction and peer acceptance. *Child Development, 52,* 171–178.

Ladd, G.W. (1983). Social networks of popular, average, and rejected children in school settings. *Merrill–Palmer Quarterly, 29,* 283–307.

LaGreca, A.M., & Santogrossi, D.A. (1980). Social skills training with elementary school students: A behavioral group approach. *Journal of Consulting and Clinical Psychology, 48,* 220–227.

Lefkowitz, M.M., & Tesiny, E.P. (1980). Assessment of childhood depression. *Journal of Consulting and Clinical Psychology, 48,* 43–50.

Maccoby, E.E., & Jacklin, C.N. (1974). *The psychology of sex differences.* Stanford, CA: Stanford University Press.

McCandless, B.R., Castaneda, A., & Palermo, D.S. (1956). Anxiety in children and social status. *Child Development, 27,* 385–391.

Meichenbaum, D., Bream, L.A., & Cohen, J.S. (in press). A cognitive-behavioral perspective of child psychopathology: Implications for assessment and training. In B. McMahon & R. Peters (Eds.), *Childhood disorders: Behavioral-developmental approaches.* New York: Brunner/Mazel.

Moore, S.G. (1967). Correlates of peer acceptance in nursery school children. *Young Children, 22,* 281–297.

Moore, S., & Updegraff, R. (1964). Sociometric status of preschool children related to age, sex, nurturance-giving, and dependency. *Child Development, 35,* 519–524.

Morrison, G.M., Forness, S.R., & MacMillan, D.L. (1983). Influences on the sociometric ratings of mildly handicapped children: A path analysis. *Journal of Educational Psychology, 75,* 63–74.

Northway, M.L. (1944). Outsiders: A study of the personality patterns of children least acceptable to their agemates. *Sociometry, 7,* 10–25.

Northway, M.L. (1946). Sociometry and some challenging problems of social relationships *Sociometry, 9,* 187–198.

Oden, S., & Asher, S.R. (1977). Coaching children in social skills for friendship making. *Child Development, 48,* 495–506.

Peery, J.C. (1979). Popular, amiable, isolated, rejected: A reconceptualization of sociometric status in preschool children. *Child Development, 50,* 1231–1234.

Peplau, L.A., Miceli, M., & Morasch, B. (1982). Loneliness and self-evaluation. In L.A. Peplau & D. Perlman (Eds.), *Loneliness: A sourcebook of current theory, research, and therapy* (pp. 135–151). New York: Wiley.

Putallaz, M. (1982, November). *The importance of the peer group for successful intervention.* Paper presented at the annual meeting of the Association for the Advancement of Behavior Therapy.

Putallaz, M., & Gottman, J. (1981). Social skills and group acceptance. In S.R. Asher & J.M. Gottman (Eds.), *The development of children's friendships* (pp. 116–149). New York: Cambridge University Press.

Putallaz, M., & Gottman, J. (1982). Conceptualizing social competence in children. In P. Karoly & J.J. Steffen (Eds.), *Improving children's competence* (pp. 1–33). Lexington, MA: Lexington Books.

Renshaw, P.D., & Asher, S.R. (1982). Social competence and peer status: The distinction between goals and strategies. In K.H. Rubin & H.S. Ross (Eds.), *Peer relationships and social skills in childhood* (pp. 375–395). New York: Springer–Verlag.

Richard, B.A., & Dodge, K.A. (1982). Social maladjustment and problem solving in school-aged children. *Journal of Consulting and Clinical Psychology, 50,* 226–233.

Riesman, D., Glazer, N., & Denney, R. (1953). *The lonely crowd.* New York: Yale University Press.

Roff, M., Sells, S.B., & Golden, M.M. (1972). *Social adjustment and personality development in children.* Minneapolis: University of Minnesota Press.

Rubin, Z. (1980). *Children's friendships.* Cambridge, MA: Harvard University Press.

Schwartz, J.C. (1972). Effects of peer familiarity on the behavior of preschoolers in a novel situation. *Journal of Personality and Social Psychology, 24,* 276–284.

Sroufe, L.A., Schork, E., Motti, F., Lawroski, N., & LaFreniere, P. (1984). The role of affect in social competence. In C.E. Izard, J. Kagan, & R.B. Zajonc (Eds.), *Emotions, cognition, and behavior* (pp. 289–319). New York: Cambridge University Press.

Thompson, G.G., & Powell, M. (1951). An investigation of the rating-scale approach to the measurement of social status. *Educational and Psychological Measurement, 11,* 440–455.

Tyne, T.F., & Flynn, J.T. (1979). The remediation of elementary students' low social status through a teacher-centered consultation program. *Journal of School Psychology, 17,* 244–254.

Vosk, B., Forehand, R., Parker, J.B., & Rickard, K. (1982). A multimethod comparison of popular and unpopular children. *Developmental Psychology, 18,* 571–575.

Waas, G.A., & French, D.C. (1984, April). *Locus of control as a mediating factor in peer social status.* Paper presented at the annual meeting of the American Educational Research Association, New Orleans.

Wheeler, V.A., & Ladd, G.W. (1982). Assessment of children's self-efficacy for social interactions with peers. *Developmental Psychology, 18,* 795–805.

5

Motivation and School Achievement

Martin L. Maehr
Jennifer Archer

University of Illinois at Urbana-Champaign

MOTIVATION AND SCHOOL ACHIEVEMENT

It has been said that as a society we are concerned, perhaps obsessed, with achievement. The media remind us repeatedly that the United States may no longer be a leader in industrial productivity and may soon lose its dominant role in science and technology. Simultaneously, there exists the fear that achievement in schools, or lack of it, may be a component in the overall picture of decline. The role of schools in contributing to the perceived crisis in achievement is unclear, although there is evidence that the public school is not all that we want it to be. Particularly disturbing is the possibility that achievement in secondary schools is not on a par with that of other highly industrialized societies, such as Japan, and that the situation may be getting worse (Harnisch, 1984).

Concerns about improving achievement prompt questions about motivation. Formal and informal observations of Japanese and American work patterns in school (Stevenson, Lee, & Ichikawa, in press) and on the job (Cole, 1979; Maehr & Braskamp, 1986; Ouchi, 1981) stress motivation as a major factor, suggesting even that the "work ethic" has been lost in our society. Current work on educational productivity stresses the role of motivation.

Estimates of the importance of motivational variables in education vary. The most sustained attention to the topic has been given by Walberg and his colleagues (Uguroglu & Walberg, 1979; Walberg, Pascarella, Haertel, Junker, & Boulanger, 1982). Generally, their findings indicate that motivation accounts for between 11 and 20% of the variance in classroom achievement. It may seem that motivation is only a minor explanatory variable, but when considered in light of other factors, this is not insignificant. The greater share of the variance is attributable to factors over which educators have little or no control, such as social background or ethnicity. The amount of variance explained by motivation, then, represents a possibility for action. Moreover, the explained variance may not be as small as Walberg's estimates suggest; his definition of motivation was a narrow one, and his procedures for assessing it were limited. As Walberg and his colleagues themselves point out, motivation cannot be ignored in the analysis of educational productivity; motivation is not the only factor, but it is a critical one (Kremer & Walberg, 1981).

The purpose of this chapter is to summarize the literature on motivation relating to achievement in the classroom. Attention also will be given to how values, ideology, and various cultural patterns impinge on classroom performance and serve to enhance motivation to achieve. The overriding question is, What can be done to promote school achievement?

MOTIVATION AND ACHIEVEMENT DEFINED

Self-evidently, motivation and achievement are important issues in a discussion of the role and work of American schools. However, it is difficult to define how motivational factors are critical to achievement, and we first must specify what is meant by them. Folklore has it that motivation concerns the inner states of the person—needs, drives, psychic energies, unconscious wishes, etc. However, we must consider more precisely the behavioral patterns that make teachers, researchers, principals, and parents think that motivation is involved in a child's behavior. When people talk about motivation, they refer to a wide variety of activities, but for the most part such talk relates to five identifiable patterns of behavior. The study of motivation begins with observations of the existence of and variations in these patterns.

1. *Direction.* An apparent choice among a set of possibilities for action is the first indicator of motivation. When a person attends to one thing and not another, we infer that he or she is motivated in a certain way. The choices that students make among behavioral alternatives suggest varying motivation (for example, when a student elects to take an after-school computer course rather than try out for the basketball team). Similarly, as one child works busily at his or her desk while another chats to a neighbor, we use the term motivation. In or out of school, it is choice among possibilities that prompts us to infer motivation.

2. *Persistence.* Persistence is the second behavioral pattern that forms the basis for inferences about motivation. When a person concentrates attention on the same task or event for extended periods of time, like a scientist hard at work in a laboratory, observers infer varying degrees of motivation.

3. *Continuing motivation.* A behavioral pattern that suggest powerful motivational forces is a return to a previously encountered task or field of work on one's own, without external constraint to do so. It is the child who

uses a free moment to do additional problems, check out an extra book to find out more about insects, or try out a new physics experiment who is thought to be motivated. Maehr and his colleagues (Fyans, Kremer, Salili, & Maehr, 1981; Maehr, 1976; Salili, Maehr, Sorensen, & Fyans, 1976; Sorensen & Maehr, 1976) have referred to this pattern as "continuing motivation" and have explicated its nature and origins, relating it to work on intrinsic motivation (Deci, 1975, 1980). While interpretable as one more index of motivation, continuing motivation takes on special significance for teachers because this sort of motivation in students is considered a crucial outcome by many educators (Maehr, 1976). While continuing motivation is similar to persistence, it has its own distinguishing characteristics. Whereas persistence is characterized by uninterrupted attention to the task, continuing motivation involves a return to a previously encountered task or field of work.

Continuing motivation, persistence, and apparent choice occur when the same direction in behavior is retained — in other words, when the person repeatedly chooses the same (or a very similar) behavioral activity while rejecting alternatives. In a sense, these three behavioral patterns are separate examples of a choice made or a behavioral direction taken.

4. *Activity.* Activity level is a fourth behavioral index of motivation. Some people seem to be more active than others. However, activity level is a more complex and less reliable indicator than choice, persistence, or continuing motivation. More so than for these three patterns, physiological factors are likely to be implicated in level of activity, complicating matters considerably. In addition, assumed differences in motivation are attributable not to activity but to direction (Maehr, 1974a). Although it may not be clear whether or not activity level is a predominant indicator of motivation in the majority of classrooms, this index nonetheless should be taken into account.

5. *Performance.* The final example of a behavioral pattern that prompts motivational inferences is variation in performance. If variation in performance cannot readily be explained in terms of variation in competence, skills, or physiological factors, then a motivational inference may be drawn. Teachers can cite instances in which "good" students fail and "bad" students show sudden improvement. Sometimes these slumps and jumps can be related to the acquisition of a necessary skill or to physiological factors such as illness. However, when these factors are not apparent, a motivational explanation may be appropriate.

Performance level is not a pure measure of motivation but a product of other factors, including a combination of motivational patterns. In other words, choice, persistence, continuing motivation, and activity level are all likely to be reflected in performance level. One might argue that such patterns provide only a crude measure of motivation, yet, perhaps because performance level is often the "bottom line" in a rationale for studying motivation, these behavioral patterns should be taken seriously. In any event, because variation in level of performance often leads to motivational inferences, this pattern finds a place in the present taxonomy.

These overlapping behavioral patterns may not be all-inclusive. They need further elaboration as specific instances and issues arise, and they need specification as better measurement and research procedures are constructed. It may be argued that they represent not observations but judgments about behavior. However, when teachers ask how they can motivate students, they are asking how they can direct students to do one thing, such as reading, and avoid other things, such as socializing, fighting, or daydreaming. Teachers also are concerned with students' persistence and hope that they engage in constructive activities not only when teachers demand them, but also in free moments at school and at home. Moreover, teachers expect that persistence and continuing motivation to attend to these activities will result in increased levels of performance. In short, motivation and behavior are intertwined, and consideration of one is impossible without consideration of the other.

Motivation as Personal Investment

While there is merit in stressing the behavioral base for motivational inferences, there also is value in considering unifying principles that might underlie these somewhat disparate behavioral patterns. The concept of personal investment has been used in discussing a wide array of activities that people pursue, the weight they place on these activities, and the direction of their lives (Maehr & Braskamp, 1986). The metaphor implicit in the term "personal investment" captures the underlying meaning of patterns associated with motivation—that is, when behavioral direction, persistence, performance, continuing motivation, and variation in activity level are observed, a person is investing his or her personal resources (time, talent, energy) in a certain way.

The image evoked by the idea of personal investment is one of *distribution*, not *availability*, of resources; the emphasis is on motivational differences rather than deprivation (Maehr, 1974a; Nicholls, 1979). This assumption of motivational differences rather than deprivation may be desirable in the study of motivation in people of varying social and cultural backgrounds Maehr & Nicholls, 1980), and similarly, such differences must be assumed in making cross-age comparisons (Maehr & Kleiber, 1981). In short, the idea of personal investment expresses the dual possibilities that people exhibit both qualitative and quantitative differences in motivation.

With this distinction in mind, it may be wise to avoid the assumption that a child is lacking in motivation and to consider the possibility that the classroom situation is not eliciting his or her effort (Maehr, 1978). However, one cannot rule out the possibility that people do vary not only in how, when, and where they are motivated, but also in their overall level of motivation.

The Motivational Cycle

The definition of motivation in terms of behavioral patterns and personal investment helps to specify motivation. It is also useful to define motivation in relation to other processes and events. One way to do this is to describe a typical motivational cycle in a particular setting. Figure 1 outlines the motivational cycle as it might exist in a classroom.

As illustrated, motivation (evidenced by choice, persistence, and activity level) is viewed as a primary antecedent of performance. However, motivation in turn is affected by the performance that eventuates and by the way this performance is appraised. Typically, motivation does not influence performance in a direct and simple manner. Other factors are involved: A person may not possess the necessary skills, the organization of the task may be overly complicated or inappropriate, and disruptive peers may hinder concentration. One can imagine both effective and ineffective effort. If the task is poorly defined or badly organized—or if the necessary tools are not available—effort may be misdirected or misused.

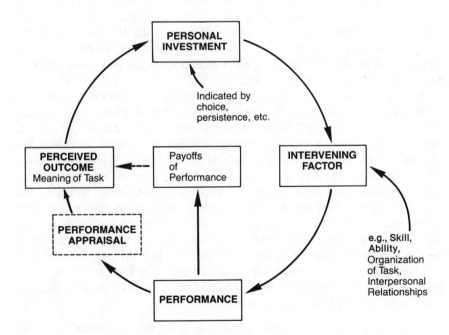

Figure 1: The motivational cycle

Another feature of the cycle concerns level of performance. While a desired level of performance may be evident to students without any input from teachers, as in the case of individualized instructional programs, often there is a process of appraisal in which significant others (teachers, parents, peers, etc.) play an evaluative role. It is the outcome as socially defined and as perceived by the student that feeds back into the motivational cycle (cf. Frieze, 1980; Frieze, Shomo, & Francis, 1979).

Payoffs for Personal Investment

The terms "motivation" and "personal investment" place no value on how people use their time, talent, and energy. Educators, however, cannot be expected to consider motivation and personal investment without focusing on payoffs. What comes from the distribution of one's personal resources? Is it good or bad? Is it equally so from different perspectives? These questions are at the heart of the issue for those concerned with school achievement: the concern is not whether the student is motivated but whether he or she is motivated in a desirable way. Many desiderata stem from an investment in the educational process; several of them are briefly described below.

Achievement.   Achievement is the first payoff of motivation. When educators worry about decreasing SAT scores, they mean school achievement; when leaders in industry worry about achievement, they mean economic productivity. Likewise, historians may consider the waxing and waning of societies in these terms. Achievement should not be defined so that this array of meanings is ignored, but it should allow for systematic analyses, both social and psychological.

For the purpose of this discussion, achievement involves observable and measurable performance that takes place in the presence of a standard of excellence. Generally, these standards are socially derived or related; achievement is considered in terms of success and failure in things that society deems valuable, such as school success or a flourishing career. Although achievement may be viewed as a characteristic of societies, groups, and institutions, we are interested primarily in individual achievement. According to this definition, the person must be an actor in an event. Finally, uncertainty of outcome is significant—behavior entered into without question of outcome is not achievement behavior. The possibility of both success and failure must exist in an achievement situation. In sum, achievement involves personal accomplishment, something that can be attributed to individual ability and effort. Also, it is something that is valued by others in addition to the performer; it has social significance.

Personal growth.   Personal growth is a second outcome of investment. Does investing oneself in a task lead to enhanced ability, skill, or competence? People do not necessarily choose tasks that increase their competence. In their spare time, some may opt to upgrade the skills they use in their work while others may choose activities that bear little relation to their professional lives. All these activities have their place, but they may have different effects on the course of a person's life, and they may "pay off" quite differently.

Life satisfaction.   Additional payoffs of motivation are satisfaction in life and mental well-being. There is the issue of matching personal investment patterns with levels of satisfaction. Patterns that end in achievement are valued by our society—but what is it that makes people happy? While the answer is elusive, any discussion of motivation and personal investment must consider affective payoffs. Does investing oneself in such a way as to excel carry with it a price in terms of long-term satisfaction? A study of highly talented performers indicates that it may. Bloom and his colleagues (Bloom, 1982a, 1982b) have studied world-class performers in music, art, sports, and science. They argue that some price in family solidarity and satisfaction is paid by these exceptional people. However, their findings indicate that extreme investment in achievement does not necessarily eventuate in deep regret, dissatisfaction, or neurotic symptoms.

DETERMINANTS OF MOTIVATION AND PERSONAL INVESTMENT

What causes people to invest themselves in certain ways? What factors influence motivation? What do we know about motivation and school performance? There are two ways to approach these questions: the first is to focus on the person and determine whether anything about previous experience helps us understand present behavior; the second is to examine factors external to the person that may influence behavior in a particular context. Because behavior always is a product of both person and situation, complex interactions occur between them.

Motivation as a Personal Trait

Perhaps the most common assumption about motivation, particularly motivation that leads to achievement, is that some people have a built-in personality trait (or traits) that leads them to productive activity. No one has explored this possibility more thoroughly than David McClelland, who, in a series of studies beginning in the 1940s, initiated a program of research that mapped out the territory for the study of motivation and achievement (McClelland, 1961, 1971, 1978, 1985; McClelland & Winter, 1969).

In his most ambitious project, McClelland (1961) examined the effect of personality on society. In brief, McClelland argued that a child is exposed to people and situations, taught things, and treated in one way rather than another. Formally and informally, often without thought or plan, he or she participates in a set of learning experiences that fosters continuing patterns. These patterns may be more or less effective in fostering achievement-related behaviors. If effective, they will create a pool of potential leaders who are achievement-motivated, and, assuming there is nothing to prevent society from drawing its leadership from this pool, an achievement-motivated leadership should come to dominate national affairs. Society as a whole therefore exhibits the characteristics of the achievement-motivated person.

While one might define social achievement more broadly, McClelland focused on economic achievement, a type relatively easy to compare across societies. Surprisingly, he did find evidence that achievement-oriented practices in child rearing were likely to eventuate in an "achieving society." This evidence consisted of correlations between the economic achievement of a society (adjusted for potential in terms of natural resources) and an index of the learning environment that would have been experienced by adults when they were children. While these correlations are not high and anomalies exist in the data, it does seem that McClelland's hypothesis is more than speculation: Society does ensure its future as it rears its children.

While McClelland's work raised many questions about motivation and achievement, it did not solve all the problems, nor does it provide a guide for research today. Ample criticism of his work is to be found elsewhere (Maehr, 1974a, 1978; Maehr & Nicholls, 1980). Nonetheless, McClelland's research emphasized the continuing and pervasive role of early learning experiences in determining how people respond to new situations. His findings underscore the possibility that some people, perhaps some groups, acquire a "motivational talent" which they exercise even as circumstances change.

Motivation and Thoughts about the Self

Generally, contemporary researchers on motivation and achievement are not inclined to think of a general motive or trait associated with achievement. Rather, their emphasis is on cognition—the thoughts, feelings, beliefs, and meanings people hold and the way these influence attitudes toward learning. Researchers have demonstrated the importance of sense of control. Deci (1975, 1980) and deCharms (1976, 1984) both stress that a person's behavior may be modified by his or her sense of initiating events rather than being controlled by them. One of the strongest predictors of achievement behavior mentioned in the Coleman report on educational equality (Coleman & Associates, 1966) was perceived locus of control, the degree to which people feel they have control over their immediate situation.

DeCharms (1976, 1984) attempted to reverse the desperate state of an inner-city school in which both students and teachers had little interest in what was going on in the classroom. By giving students a degree of choice over what they were doing, as well as responsibility for the outcome, de-Charms attempted to teach them to think of themselves as determiners of their own behavior. He reasoned that, if students felt they were in control of their behavior in school, they would be more prepared to study. However, he found it impossible to change the behavior of the students without changing that of their teachers. Conditions had to be altered so that teachers, as well as students, felt like "origins" rather than "pawns" within the system. As teachers developed a sense of being in control of their teaching, they were able to transfer a similar belief to their students. Thus, a belief in self-determination, coupled with a sense of ownership, was important in enhancing student morale and achievement.

Bernard Weiner (1979, 1984) proposed that achievement motivation could be understood in terms of attributions, that is, the causal judgments people make following personal experiences of success or failure. In an early study (Weiner & Kukla, 1970), Weiner demonstrated that people who scored high on a measure of achievement motivation attributed their success to something they personally had done rather than to luck or to ease of the task. Conversely, they attributed failure to external factors. People who scored low on the measure of motivation showed a contrasting pattern in which failure was attributed to internal factors such as a lack of ability and success was attributed externally. During the last 15 years or so, a large body of research has been built upon Weiner's pioneering work in attribution theory. Researchers have concerned themselves with the causes people assign to their successes and failures in academic situations and with how these attributions in turn affect behavior.

While this focus on attributions has highlighted the importance of the immediate situation on motivation, consideration also should be given to the proposition, emphasized by McClelland, that experience imbeds itself in enduring behavioral predispositions. Early experiences, both in and out of school, influence how children feel about their abilities and about the relevance and value of activities. These feelings are critical antecedents of achievement. It seems clear that people who are confident in their ability to achieve will seek out and perform tasks that serve to challenge and enhance that ability (Fyans & Maehr, 1979; Maehr & Willig, 1982). Similarly, negative judgments about one's ability to succeed produce patterns of behavior that work toward fulfilling negative outcomes. Children's judgments about their ability have been found to be already well established by the fourth grade (Fyans & Maehr, 1979).

Motivation and Achievement Goals

Carol Dweck and her colleagues (Dweck, 1975, 1984; Dweck & Bempechat, 1983; Dweck & Elliott, 1983) have proposed two classes of achievement goals: learning goals and performance goals. People who hold learning goals, Dweck asserts, are concerned with their competence in performing a task and look for ways of increasing mastery of it. They adopt personal standards of success rather than external normative standards, and expect that they will achieve success with expenditure of effort. They feel in control of the situation and derive satisfaction from task completion.

People with performance goals, on the other hand, are concerned with validating their competence and with obtaining favorable judgments of their competence, or at least avoiding unfavorable ones. They endorse external, normative standards of success and failure that involve evaluation of performance relative to that of others. In order to "win," they may select tasks in which there is a high likelihood of outperforming others. This may mean choosing a less challenging task over a more challenging one or selecting a task of little intrinsic interest if it offers a high possibility of success. Although people can modify their own behavior, they cannot change the behavior of others, nor can they establish the criteria used to evaluate performance. As a result, people with performance goals may feel little sense of personal control. Success is likely to be attributed to the possession of ability rather than the expenditure of effort, and a sense of satisfaction comes from the validation of the possession of ability. Dweck argues that, while people can hold both learning and performance goals simultaneously, sometimes conflicts occur and a choice between them must be made.

Value Attached to the Task

While research has focused on subjective judgments about one's ability and the goals one holds, the value of the task likewise is important. McClelland (1961) emphasized the value component in achievement, particularly in relation to differences among societies and sociocultural groups. This point also has been stressed by others (Fyans et al., 1981; Maehr, 1978; Parsons & Goff, 1980; Triandis & Brislin, 1980; Triandis & Associates, 1973) but has not been as thoroughly researched as one might expect. Perhaps because it seems self-evident that one does what one values, few have analyzed the concept of valuing as a psychological process or have related valuing to differential achievement patterns. In a study by Willig, Harnisch, Hill, and Maehr (1983), it was found that the achievement of black students was more attributable to the value they placed on school tasks than to their perceptions of their ability.

In reviewing research on personality and motivation, several conclusions are apparent. First, it is difficult to ignore a continuing effect of previous experience on the way one approaches achievement situations. In particular, beliefs about oneself as adequate to perform tasks are critical, as are acquired goals and beliefs about what is valuable. These basic motivational orientations often are formed early in life outside schools and are not always amenable to change by teachers, though some intervention programs have proven successful (deCharms, 1976, 1984; Kleiber & Maehr, in press; McClelland & Winter, 1969).

Situational Influences on Motivation

Although a person's previous experiences affect motivation, past experience alone does not determine present motivational patterns. Extensive research has been devoted to determining the characteristics of situations that affect motivation — in particular, social expectations, school characteristics, the nature of the task, dimensions of the task, and the structure of the learning environment.

Social expectations. People do not act in isolation from the social groups to which they belong. These groups in large part determine for their members what is worth doing and what is expected of each of them. Expectations or norms define options for behavior: where, how, and to what degree people should invest their time, talent, and energy.

In addition, the roles that members play are accompanied by different expectations for performance. Equally interesting is the effect on motivation and performance of filling a social role. Even the temporary assignment of a leadership role, for example, seems to be followed by increased achievement motivation (Zander & Forward, 1968). Within the social group, higher status people seem to be encouraged to achieve, whereas lower status people are discouraged (Maehr, 1974a, 1974b, 1978). In sum, a person's place among peers has important effects on motivation — change the situation, the peers, or both, and motivation often changes, sometimes drastically so.

A second type of expectation is conveyed by significant others, such as teachers. Teacher expectations have been a focus of research for several years (Brophy, 1983, 1985; Cooper, 1979, 1983; Peterson & Barger, 1985). This research suggests that the expectations teachers hold affect the quality of the interactions they initiate with students. These expectations are not always conscious and sometimes are invalid. What is disturbing is the evidence that expectations can serve as self-fulfilling prophecies. Weiner and Kukla (1970) suggest, for example, that teachers fulfill expectations when they attribute student performance to ability, effort, task difficulty, or luck. Teachers are in the business of evaluating performance and, perhaps unwittingly, they teach students about the causes of success or failure. However, by failing to monitor the relationship between their own expectations and the ways they interact with students, teachers may set low performance standards for students who are capable of more. One example of this phenomenon has been reported by Perry (1975), who demonstrated that teachers provide more probing types of feedback when they hold high expectations for students. Interactions between teacher and student can have a cumulative effect and may penalize the student who fails to make an early impression as a potential high achiever.

School characteristics. In recent years, there has been growing interest in the effectiveness of schools, spurred not only by falling scores on standardized tests but also by fears that students are failing to develop a long-term desire for learning and lack the ability to adapt in a rapidly changing environment. Researchers have demonstrated that the way schools are organized can affect students' productivity (D'Amico, 1982; Deal & Kennedy, 1983; Good & Brophy, in press; Sergiovanni, 1984). It seems that effective schools have developed a climate or "culture" that supports academic achievement. Many factors affect this climate — for example, leadership, curricular organization, administrative and teaching practices, and environmental characteristics. Researchers have been seeking to identify the most salient of these.

Purkey and Smith (1982) stress the need for dynamic leadership and high expectations for student performance. We have considered already the impact of teacher expectations on students' behavior and have mentioned the dangers of setting expectations too low. The role of the principal in an effective school is at least twofold: first, to act as a figurehead, a focus that unites the disparate elements of the school and emphasizes its common goals; and second, to work actively with teachers and students, helping and encouraging them to achieve those goals.

Task dimensions. The task itself also may be a significant determinant of motivation. First, the task may have structural features that affect motivation. For example, some tasks are more interesting than others. Why this is true is not clear, but research on intrinsic motivation suggests that a task possessing an optimum level of uncertainty and unpredictability tends to be attractive (Deci, 1975). It appears that there is a built-in attraction to these features in tasks.

Second, a task may have specific meaning in a particular sociocultural context. Is it an acceptable area in which to perform? One's social or cultural group may define the task as desirable, undesirable, or irrelevant. Barkow (1976) points out that the prestige ranking of a task within a cultural group may by itself best explain the motivation exhibited by members of the group. Further, tasks may be viewed as instrumental to valued ends, and success in their performance may confirm one's identity or enhance one's self-view (Maehr, 1974b).

Third is the issue of performance appraisal. The way appraisals are carried out may have far-reaching and unintended consequences. For example, studies have indicated that placing emphasis on testing and on teachers' evaluation of performance can have negative effects on student motivation (Fyans et al., 1981; Hill, 1980, 1984; Maehr, 1976; Salili et al., 1976). While an emphasis on external evaluation momentarily may enhance performance, it may negatively affect continuing motivation by ruling out the establishment of more intrinsic, task-related goals (Maehr, 1976).

Similar to and perhaps implicit in the issue of evaluation and performance appraisal is the degree of freedom and choice that can be allowed in the performance of a task. Wang and Stiles (1976) conducted an investigation in which the effects of student selection and teacher selection of schoolwork schedules were compared (see also Wang, 1981). Results indicated that students were more likely to complete assignments in the former condition than in the latter. As described earlier, deCharms (1976), demonstrated improved productivity and enhanced motivation when students participated in planning their academic program. A study by Pascarella, Walberg, Junker, and Haertel (1981) demonstrated the importance of freedom in learning. While teacher control was associated positively with science achievement for both younger and older adolescent students, it was associated negatively with a measure of continuing motivation in science. Apparently, educational conditions that emphasize control of student behavior may produce desirable effects of a short-term nature but may discourage continuing motivation.

Learning structure. Carole Ames and her colleagues (Ames, 1978, 1981, 1984; Ames & Ames, 1981; Ames, Ames, & Felker, 1977; Ames & Felker, 1979; Ames & McKelvie, 1982) have investigated the effects of different goal structures on students' motivational patterns. They examined three different situations: first, a competitive structure in which the goal was to complete a task better or faster than others; second, a cooperative structure in which students worked together to complete a common task; and third, an individualistic structure in which students worked singly, setting individual goals and trying to improve upon their past performances. In Ames' experiments, the impositions of the different goal structures appeared to trigger different motivational patterns in students—they paid attention to different cues, made different attributions following success and failure, devised different strategies to complete tasks, and made different self-evaluations.

Briefly, the imposition of a competitive goal structure prompted students to compare their performance with that of their peers, to make attributions about the presence or absence of ability, and to be concerned with questions about "smartness" and their capability of completing a task. Imposition of a cooperative goal structure prompted students to consider their individual performance in relation to that of the group as a whole. A sense of moral responsibility, the need to work hard so as not to "let down" the group, was generated. The individualistic goal structure focused students' attention on their present task and on the amount of effort necessary to improve on prior performance. The emphasis was on mastery and, to this end, on devising strategies to complete the task.

Like the work on school effectiveness, Ames' research suggests another way in which students' motivation to achieve may be enhanced. Within classrooms, teachers may be able to reduce a competitive orientation, with its deleterious consequences for less able students, and impose in its place an approach that encourages students' desire to master tasks and promotes interest in learning for its own sake.

Summary

In general, research has shown that factors both internal and external to the person influence motivation to achieve. Internal factors include McClelland's early notion of motivation as a trait of personality as well as more current emphases on cognitions, or the way a person's beliefs, values, goals, and sense of being in control of a situation spur different motivations and patterns of behavior. Situational influences on students' motivation include expectations held by relevant social groups and, more directly, by teachers. School effectiveness — that is, viewing motivation at the level of the school as a whole — is also important. Characteristics of the task itself include structure, meaning, and appraisal. Finally, different motivational patterns may be triggered by the imposition of different goal structures. It must be stressed that not one but many of these factors operate to enhance or diminish motivation to achieve. In the next section, personal investment theory (Maehr, 1984; Maehr & Braskamp, 1986) will be described in more detail to provide a basis for combining many of these factors into a coherent whole.

PERSONAL INVESTMENT: AN INTERPRETATION

In assessing school achievement, it may be helpful to bear in mind the concept of personal investment, which suggests that motivation is demonstrated by individual choices and which indicates further that performance "problems" should not necessarily be attributed to a lack of motivation. For example, the child who is considered unmotivated in class may be choosing not to direct attention to the task at hand. In another context, he or she may show all the energy that generally characterizes motivation. In a situation in which the child exhibits little motivation, the parent or teacher might well consider what it is about the task that is not eliciting the child's attention.

Meaning and Personal Investment

The meaning of the situation to the person involved is critical; it determines how the participant chooses to invest himself or herself. Three types of perceptions or cognitions are particularly salient in forming meaning: first, the perception of options or action possibilities; second, views of oneself in relation to the situation, especially the view of oneself as capable of performing competently; and third, personal goals or incentives that spur behavior.

Perceived options. Perceived options refer to the behavioral alternatives that a person sees as available. That is, within a particular environment, some behaviors are more feasible than others. A boy growing up within an Amish community is more likely to become a farmer than a cabaret performer. In addition to what is perceived to be available, a person will have a perception of what is socially and culturally appropriate. Playing with a computer is not an option for many students from poor families, even though they may have seen one and know a bit about its properties. In any consideration of people's choice of behavior, the relevance of the behavior within their world is paramount. This is evident in the case of elite performers (Bloom, 1982a, 1982b). They were born into families who valued a particular activity, promoted and rewarded it, and knew how to facilitate achievement in it. Although not all children in such families develop their talent to the same degree, the opportunity must exist for the development of outstanding performance.

Sense of self. Given possibilities for action, what determines the precise course a person will take? As indicated earlier, recent research on motivation and achievement has moved away from a notion of a general motive or motivational orientation at the source of achievement behavior. Emphasis now is placed on judgments that people make about themselves in relation to a perceived situation. Four components of selfhood may figure in motivation: self-identity, self-reliance, goal-directedness, and sense of competence. People have a sense of identity when they feel themselves to be part of social groups. Self-identity affects knowledge about and acceptance of social expectations and individual purposes and goals. Self-identity not only defines what is worth striving for but also defines how striving should occur.

Self-reliance concerns the perceived origin of events. Does the individual initiate events, or are they prompted by other people, things, or situations? As a rule, the perception that one plays a causal role in the outcome of an event is followed by increased effort. This perception of control is associated with intrinsic motivation, or increased effort that ensues apart from extrinsic rewards. In fact, extrinsic rewards appear to militate against the perception that one is an initiator, and the use of extrinsic rewards often subverts intrinsic interests and independent motivation (Lepper & Greene, 1978).

As defined by Maehr and Braskamp (1986), goal-directedness refers to the tendency to set goals and organize one's behavior accordingly. The person feels that he or she is *becoming* something rather than just *being* something (Allport, 1955). This category encompasses such components of achievement over the long term as the ability to delay gratification (Mischel, 1974).

Sense of competence refers to subjective judgments people make about their ability to perform, or the judgment that they can or cannot do something. This judgment varies in degree and extent—it may be limited to one area or generalized across a variety of domains. This component of self is probably the one most often associated with achievement motivation (Covington, 1984; Kukla, 1978; Nicholls, 1983, 1984; Roberts, 1984a, 1984b).

Personal incentives.   How perceptions of self affect motivation and achievement depends on the incentives people have. An incentive refers to the motivational focus of an activity: What does the person expect to get out of performing? What is the value of the activity? More concretely, how do people define success and failure in the situation? While one might imagine an infinite number of incentives, four categories seem to influence achievement patterns (Maehr, 1984; Maehr & Braskamp, 1986): task, ego, social solidarity, and extrinsic rewards.

Task personal incentives embrace two somewhat different purposes in performance. First is the performance situation described by Csikszentmihalyi (1975, 1978), in which the person is absorbed totally in a task and social comparisons of performance are remote or nonexistent. Second is the desire to demonstrate competence, initially described by White (1959, 1960) and currently the object of considerable research (e.g., Harter, 1980, 1982; Harter & Connell, 1983).

Ego personal incentives refer to concerns about doing better than a socially defined standard, especially doing better than others. Whereas task-oriented incentives are, at most, self-competitive, ego incentives are explicitly socially competitive (Maehr & Sjogren, 1971). Achieving an ego incentive involves beating someone, doing better than another, winning, being the best. Nor surprisingly, sense of competence becomes particularly important when ego incentives are salient.

Social solidarity incentives refer to the desire to gain social approval for one's behavior. Although these incentives are not always thought of in terms of achievement, pleasing significant others is a critical factor in many classrooms. For example, students may wish to demonstrate to the teacher that they have good intentions, mean well, try hard, and in this sense are "good" boys or girls. Demonstrating good intentions is a means of gaining social approval. When one holds a social solidarity incentive, demonstrating faithfulness is more important than doing the task for its own sake or showing that one is better than someone else.

Extrinsic rewards refer to incentives associated with earning money, prizes, or some other object of value not inherent in the performance of the task itself. Such rewards usually are alien to the task and to the person's reasons for performing it. In fact, it may be more appropriate to view these incentives not as ends in themselves but as subgoals whose attainment facilitates other personal and more intrinsic incentives. Work on the social psychology of extrinsic/intrinsic motivation (Deci, 1975, 1980; Harter, 1980; Lepper & Greene, 1978) has made it clear that external rewards do play a role in achievement.

Conditions Affecting Perceived Options, Sense of Self, and Personal Incentives

While perceived options, sense of self, and personal incentives may be viewed as mediating factors that determine motivation and personal investment, what factors or events are antecedent to these perceptions? How does a person come to view himself or herself and a specific situation in a way that elicits greater or lesser effort?

One may think of meaning and personal investment as having their source in the dual factors of situation and person as well as in a complex of person/situation interactions. Figure 2 outlines some of the major factors that are likely to be important in this regard. Specifically, there are four antecedent categories: task design, personal experience, instruction, and sociocultural context. Underlying these categories are developmental/maturational factors—it is evident that cognitive development plays a major role in modifying the function of these factors. More directly, external factors affect the components of meaning differentially. Previous learning and personal experience are likely to have a major impact on sense of self, whereas instructional programs and the broader sociocultural milieu are important in defining perceived options. For example, a teacher's stressing learning for learning's sake (Dweck, 1984; Nicholls, 1979, 1984), or competition (Ames, 1978, 1981, 1984; Ames, Ames, & Felker, 1977; Dweck, 1984; Hill, 1980, 1984), or interpersonal relationships (Johnson & Johnson, 1979; Slavin, 1983) will likely affect students' goals for classroom performance.

CONCLUSION

As noted at the beginning of this chapter, there is a pervasive concern with the effectiveness of our public schools. Numerous journal articles, newspa-

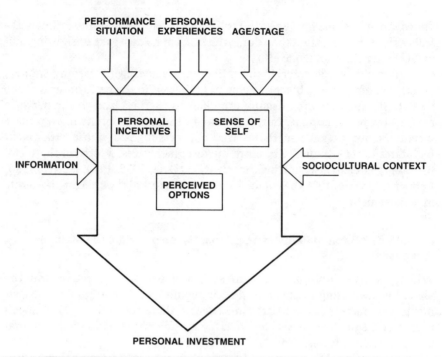

Figure 2: Antecedents of meaning and personal investment

per reports, books, and governmental commissions have presented both fact and opinion on this issue. This chapter offers yet more material, but it is material undergirded by considerable research evidence.

Whether or not the claims of a marked decline in the quality of schools are justified, few would disagree with the proposition that schools can be improved. Those with the responsibility for effecting change should consider the role that motivation plays in determining the effectiveness of schooling and student achievement. Motivation is not the only cause of variation in student achievement, but it is an important one. Moreover, student motivation can be influenced by teachers and, more generally, by the "culture" of the school. Though students arrive at new situations with "experiential baggage" that affects how they behave, it is clear that the way learning tasks are defined, expectations are established, and goals are set also make a difference in students' performance. In this chapter, current research on motivation as it relates to achievement and school effectiveness has been briefly summarized.

From this summary, a theory of personal investment stressing the role of cognitive mediators in determining motivation was developed. The stress on cognition suggests that motivation can be changed by what is done in the immediate situation: the way materials are presented, the way classrooms and schools are managed, the way learning tasks are organized, and the way students are treated. At the heart of personal investment theory is the contention that students invest themselves in learning tasks as they see meaning in those tasks. Much more remains to be done in identifying more precisely what teachers and administrators can do to enhance meaning for students and thus encourage their personal investment in academic achievement.

REFERENCES

Allport, G.W. (1955). *Becoming: Basic considerations for a psychology of personality.* New Haven, CT: Yale University Press.

Ames, C. (1978). Children's achievement attributions and self-reinforcement: Effects of self-concept and competitive reward structure. *Journal of Educational Psychology, 70,* 345-355.

Ames, C. (1981). Competitive versus cooperative reward structures: The influence of individual and group performance factors on achievement attributions and affect. *American Educational Research Journal, 18,* 273-287.

Ames, C. (1984). Competitive, cooperative, and individualistic goal structures: A cognitive-instructional analysis. In R. Ames & C. Ames (Eds.), *Motivation in education, Vol. 1: Student motivation* (pp. 177-207). New York: Academic.

Ames, C., & Ames, R. (1981). Competitive versus individualistic goal structures: The salience of past performance information for causal attributions and affect. *Journal of Educational Psychology, 73,* 411-418.

Ames, C., Ames, R., & Felker, D.W. (1977). Effects of competitive reward structure and valence of outcome on children's achievement attributions. *Journal of Educational Psychology, 69,* 1-8.

Ames, C., & Felker, D. (1979). An examination of children's attributions and achievement-related evaluations in competitive, cooperative, and individualistic reward structures. *Journal of Educational Psychology, 71,* 413-420.

Ames, C., & McKelvie, S. (1982, April). *Evaluation of student achievement behavior within cooperative and competitive reward structures.* Paper presented at the meeting of the American Educational Research Association, New York.

Barkow, J.W. (1976). Attention structure and the evolution of human psychological characteristics. In M.R.A. Chance & R.R. Larsen (Eds.), *The social structure of attention* (pp. 203-219). New York: Wiley.

Bloom, B.S. (1982a). The master teachers. *Phi Delta Kappan, 63,* 664-668.

Bloom, B.S. (1982b). The role of gifts and markers in the development of talent. *Exceptional Children, 48,* 510-522.

Brophy, J.E. (1983). Research on the self-fulfilling prophecy and teacher expectations. *Journal of Educational Psychology, 75,* 631-661.

Brophy, J.E. (1985). Teachers' expectations, motives, and goals for working with problem students. In C. Ames & R. Ames (Eds.), *Research on motivation in education, Vol. 2: The classroom milieu* (pp. 179-214). New York: Academic.

Cole, R.E. (1979). *Work, mobility, and participation: A comparative study of American and Japanese industry.* Berkeley: University of California Press.

Coleman, J.S., & Associates (1966). *Equality of educational opportunity.* Washington, DC: U.S. Government Printing Office. (ERIC Document Reproduction Service No. ED 012 275)

Cooper, H.M. (1979). Pygmalion grows up: A model for teacher expectation communication and performance influence. *Review of Educational Research, 49,* 389-410.

Cooper, H.M. (1983). Communication of teacher expectations to students. In J. Levine & M. Wang (Eds.), *Teacher and student perceptions* (pp. 193–211). Hillsdale, NJ: Erlbaum.

Covington, M.V. (1984). The motive for self-worth. In R. Ames & C. Ames (Eds.), *Research on motivation in education, Vol. 1: Student motivation* (pp. 77–112). New York: Academic.

Csikszentmihalyi, M. (1975). *Beyond boredom and anxiety.* San Francisco: Jossey-Bass.

Csikszentmihalyi, M. (1978). Intrinsic rewards and emergent motivation. In M.R. Lepper & D. Greene (Eds.), *The hidden costs of rewards* (pp. 205–216). Hillsdale, NJ: Erlbaum.

Csikszentmihalyi, M. (1985). Emergent motivation and the evolution of the self. In D.A. Kleiber & M.L. Maehr (Eds.), *Advances in motivation and achievement, Vol. 4: Motivation and adulthood* (pp. 93–119). Greenwich, CT: JAI Press.

D'Amico, J.J. (1982). Each effective school may be one of a kind. *Educational Leadership, 40*(3), 61–62.

Deal, T.E., & Kennedy, A.A. (1983). Culture and school performance. *Educational Leadership, 40,* 14–15.

deCharms, R. (1976). *Enhancing motivation: Change in the classroom.* New York: Irvington.

deCharms, R. (1984). Motivation enhancement in educational settings. In R. Ames & C. Ames (Eds.), *Motivation in education, Vol. 1: Student motivation* (pp. 275–310). New York: Academic.

Deci, E.L. (1975). *Intrinsic motivation.* New York: Plenum.

Deci, E.L. (1980). *The psychology of self-determination.* Lexington, MA: Heath.

Dweck, C.S. (1975). The role of expectations and attributions in the alleviation of learned helplessness. *Journal of Personality and Social Psychology, 31,* 674–685.

Dweck, C.S. (1984). Motivation. In R. Glaser & A. Lesgold (Eds.), *The handbook of psychology and education* (Vol. 1). Hillsdale, NJ: Erlbaum.

Dweck, C.S., & Bempechat, J. (1983). Children's theories of intelligence: Impact on learning. In S.G. Paris, G.M. Olson, & H.W. Stevenson (Eds.), *Learning and motivation in the classroom* (pp. 239–256). Hillsdale, NJ: Erlbaum.

Dweck, C.S., & Elliott, E.S. (1983). Achievement motivation. In P. Mussen & E.M. Hetherington (Eds.), *Handbook of child psychology* (Vol. 4, pp. 643–691). New York: Wiley.

Frieze, I.H. (1980). Beliefs about success and failure in the classroom. In J.H. McMillen (Ed.), *The social psychology of school learning* (pp. 39–78). New York: Academic.

Frieze, I.H., Shomo, K.H., & Francis, W.D. (1979, October). *Determinants of subjective feelings of success.* Paper presented at the Learning Research Development Center conference, Teacher and student perceptions of success and failure: Implications for learning, Pittsburgh.

Fyans, L.J., Jr., Kremer, B., Salili, F., & Maehr, M.L. (1981). The effects of evaluation conditions on continuing motivation: A study of the cultural, personological, and situational antecedents of a motivational pattern. *International Journal of Intercultural Relations, 5,* 1–22.

Fyans, L.J., Jr., & Maehr, M.L. (1979). Attributional style, task selection, and achievement. *Journal of Educational Psychology, 71,* 499–507.

Good, T., & Brophy, J.E. (in press). The school effectiveness literature: A review of research. In T. Husen & T.N. Postlethwaite (Eds.), *International encyclopedia of education.* Oxford, England: Pergamon.

Harnisch, D.L. (1984, March). *A comparison of educational productivity factors in mathematics for high school students from Japan and Illinois.* Paper presented at the meeting of the American Educational Research Association, New Orleans.

Harter, S. (1980). A model of intrinsic mastery motivation in children: Individual differences and developmental change. In W.A. Collins (Ed.), *Minnesota symposium in child psychology* (Vol. 14, pp. 215–255). Hillsdale, NJ: Erlbaum.

Harter, S. (1982). Developmental perspectives in the self-system. In P. Mussen & E.M. Hetherington (Eds.), *Handbook of child psychology* (Vol. 4, pp. 275–385). New York: Wiley.

Harter, S., & Connell, J.P. (1983). A structural model of the relationships among children's academic achievement and their self-perceptions of competence, control and motivational orientation in the cognitive domain. In J. Nicholls (Ed.), *Advances in motivation and achievement, Vol. 3: The development of achievement motivation* (pp. 219–250). Greenwich, CT: JAI.

Hill, K.T. (1980). Motivation, evaluation, and testing policy. In L.J. Fyans, Jr. (Ed.), *Achievement motivation: Recent trends in theory and research* (pp. 34–95). New York: Plenum.

Hill, K.T. (1984). Debilitating motivation and testing: A major educational problem — possible solutions and policy applications. In R. Ames & C. Ames (Eds.), *Research on motivation in education, Vol. 1: Student motivation* (pp. 245–274). New York: Academic.

Johnson, D., & Johnson, R. (1979). Cooperation, competition, and individualization. In H. Walberg (Ed.), *Educational environments and effects* (pp. 101–119). Berkeley, CA: McCutchan.

Kleiber, D.A., & Maehr, M.L. (Eds.). (in press). *Advances in motivation and achievement, Vol. 5: Enhancing motivation.* Greenwich, CT: JAI.

Kremer, B.K., & Walberg, H.J. (1981). A synthesis of social and psychological influences on science learning. *Science Education, 65,* 11–23.

Kukla, A. (1978). An attributional theory of choice. In L. Berkowitz (Ed.), *Advances in experimental social psychology* (Vol. 11). New York: Academic.

Lepper, M.R., & Greene, D. (Eds.). (1978). *The hidden costs of reward: New perspectives on the psychology of human motivation.* Hillsdale, NJ: Erlbaum.

Maehr, M.L. (1974a). Culture and achievement motivation. *American Psychologist, 29,* 887–896.

Maehr, M.L. (1974b). *Sociocultural origins of achievement.* Monterey, CA: Brooks/Cole.

Maehr, M.L. (1976). Continuing motivation: An analysis of a seldom considered educational outcome. *Review of Educational Research, 46,* 443–462.

Maehr, M.L. (1978). Sociocultural origins of achievement. In D. Bar–Tal & L. Saxe (Eds.), *Social psychology of education: Theory and research* (pp. 205–227). New York: Wiley.

Maehr, M.L. (1984). Meaning and motivation. In R. Ames & C. Ames (Eds.), *Research on motivation in education, Vol. 1: Student motivation* (pp. 115–144). New York: Academic.

Maehr, M.L., & Braskamp, L.A. (1986). *The motivation factor: A theory of personal investment.* Lexington, MA: Heath.

Maehr, M.L., & Kleiber, D.A. (1981). The graying of achievement motivation. *American Psychologist, 36,* 787–793.

Maehr, M.L., & Nicholls, J.G. (1980). Culture and achievement motivation: A second look. In N. Warren (Ed.), *Studies in cross-cultural psychology* (Vol. 3). New York: Academic.

Maehr, M.L., & Sjogren, D. (1971). Atkinson's theory of achievement motivation: First step toward a theory of academic motivation? *Review of Educational Research, 41,* 143–161.

Maehr, M.L., & Willig, A.C. (1982). Students. In H. Walberg (Ed.), *Improving educational standards and productivity* (pp. 111–124). Berkeley, CA: McCutchan.

McClelland, D.C. (1961). *The achieving society.* New York: Free Press.

McClelland, D.C. (1971). *Motivational trends in society.* New York: General Learning.

McClelland, D.C. (1978). Managing motivation to expand human freedom. *American Psychologist, 33,* 201–210.

McClelland, D.C. (1985). *Human motivation.* Glenview, IL: Scott Foresman.

McClelland, D.C., & Winter, D.G. (1969). *Motivating economic achievement.* New York: Free Press.

Mischel, W. (1974). Processes in delay of gratification. In L. Berkowitz (Ed.). *Advances in experimental social psychology* (Vol. 7). New York: Academic.

Nicholls, J.G. (1979). Quality and inequality in intellectual development: The role of motivation in education. *American Psychologist, 34,* 1071–1084.

Nicholls, J.G. (1983). Conceptions of ability and achievement motivation: A theory and its implications for education. In S.G. Paris, G.M. Olson, & H.W. Stevenson (Eds.), *Learning and motivation in the classroom* (pp. 211–237). Hillsdale, NJ: Erlbaum.

Nicholls, J.G. (1984). Conceptions of ability and achievement motivation. In R. Ames & C. Ames (Eds.), *Research on motivation in education, Vol. 1: Student motivation* (pp. 39–73). New York: Academic.

Ouchi, W. (1981). *Theory Z corporations: How American business can meet the Japanese challenge.* Reading, MA: Addison–Wesley.

Parsons, J.E., & Goff, S.B. (1980). Achievement motivation and values: An alternative perspective. In L.J. Fyans, Jr. (Ed.), *Achievement motivation* (pp. 349–373). New York: Plenum.

Pascarella, E.T., Walberg, H.J., Junker, L.K., & Haertel, G.D. (1981). Continuing motivation in science for early and late adolescents. *American Educational Research Journal, 18,* 439–452.

Perry, E. (1975, September). *Communication of teacher expectations over time.* Paper presented at a meeting of the American Psychological Association, Chicago.

Peterson, P.L., & Barger, S.A. (1985). Attribution theory and teacher expectancy. In J.B. Dusek (Ed.), *Teacher expectancies* (pp. 159–184). Hillsdale, NJ: Erlbaum.

Purkey, S.C., & Smith, M.S. (1982). Too soon to cheer? Synthesis of research on effective schools. *Educational Leadership, 40*(3), 64–69.

Roberts, G.C. (1984a). Achievement motivation in children's sport. In J.G. Nicholls (Ed.), *Advances in motivation and achievement, Vol. 3: The development of achievement motivation* (pp. 251–281). Greenwich, CT: JAI.

Roberts, G.C. (1984b). Achievement motivation and sport behavior. In R. Terjung (Ed.), *Exercise sport science review.* Philadelphia: Franklin Institute Press.

Salili, F., Maehr, M.L., Sorensen, R.L., & Fyans, L.J., Jr. (1976). A further consideration of the effects of evaluation on motivation. *American Educational Research Journal, 13,* 85–102.

Sergiovanni, T.J. (1984). Leadership and excellence in schooling. *Educational Leadership, 41*(5), 4–13.

Slavin, R. (1983). *Cooperative learning.* New York: Longman.

Sorensen, R.L., & Maehr, M.L. (1976). Toward the experimental analysis of "continuing motivation." *Journal of Educational Research, 69,* 319–322.

Stevenson, H., Lee, S., & Ichikawa, F. (in press). Attitudes and achievement: Chinese, Japanese and American children. In D.A. Kleiber & M.L. Maehr (Eds.), *Advances in motivation and achievement, Vol. 5: Enhancing motivation.* Greenwich, CT: JAI.

Triandis, H.C., & Brislin, R.W. (Eds.). (1980). *Handbook of cross-cultural psychology* (Vol. 2). New York: Allyn & Bacon.

Triandis, H.C., & Associates (1973). *The analysis of subjective culture.* New York: Wiley.

Uguroglu, M.E., & Walberg, H.J. (1979). Motivation and achievement: A quantitative synthesis. *American Educational Research Journal, 16,* 375–389.

Walberg, H.J., Pascarella, E., Haertel, G., Junker, L., & Boulanger, D. (1982). Probing a model of educational productivity with national assessment samples. *Journal of Educational Psychology, 74,* 285–307.

Wang, M.C. (1981). Development and consequences of students' sense of personal control. In J. Levine & M.C. Wang (Eds.), *Teacher and student perceptions: Implications for learning* (pp. 213–247). Hillsdale, NJ: Erlbaum.

Wang, M.C., & Stiles, B. (1976). An investigation of children's concept of self responsibility for their school learning. *American Educational Research Journal, 13,* 159–179.

Weiner, B. (1979). A theory of motivation for some classroom experiences. *Journal of Educational Psychology, 71,* 3–25.

Weiner, B. (1984). Principles for a theory of student motivation and their application within an attributional framework. In R. Ames & C. Ames (Eds.), *Research on motivation in education, Vol. 1: Student motivation* (pp. 15–38). New York: Academic.

Weiner, B., & Kukla, A. (1970). An attributional analysis of achievement motivation. *Journal of Personality and Social Psychology, 15,* 1–20.

White, R. W. (1959). Motivation reconsidered: The concept of competence. *Psychological Review, 66,* 297–333.

White, R.W. (1960). Competence and the psychosexual stages of development. In M.R. Jones (Ed.), *Nebraska symposium on motivation* (pp. 97–140). Lincoln: University of Nebraska Press.

Willig, A.C., Harnisch, D.L., Hill, K.T., & Maehr, M.L. (1983). Sociocultural and educational correlates of success–failure attributions and evaluation anxiety in the school setting for Black, Hispanic, and Anglo children. *American Educational Research Journal, 20,* 385–410.

Zander, A., & Forward, J. (1968). Position in group, achievement motivation, and group aspirations. *Journal of Personality and Social Psychology, 8,* 282–288.

AUTHOR NOTE

This chapter is based on a paper prepared by Martin L. Maehr and commissioned by the National Commission on Excellence in Education (NIE 400-81-0004, Task 10), December 1982.

6

Toward an Interactional Model of Developmental Changes in Social Pretend Play

Artin Göncü

University of Utah

The conceptualization of children's play is entering a new phase. During the last 50 years, pretend play has been investigated in terms of its social structure. Influenced by Parten (1932), much effort has been devoted to the identification of various categories of social participation. Such categories include parallel, associative, and cooperative play forms (Rubin, Fein, & Vandenberg, 1983). Studies based on such a categorical framework have revealed that social pretend play becomes increasingly organized and cooperative with age (e.g., McLoyd, Thomas, & Warren, 1984; Rubin, Maioni, & Hornung, 1976; Rubin, Watson, & Jambor, 1978).

However, the categorical approach has left open the investigation of ways in which children achieve cooperation in pretend play. Increasing emphasis is now being placed on how children develop mutually meaningful representation of objects, events, and identities (Göncü, 1984; Göncü & Kessel, 1984; Wolf, 1984). In this dynamic view, social pretend play is conceptualized as an unfolding process of seeking and reaching consensus among play partners (Kelly-Byrne, 1984). The dynamic analysis of play extends the categorical approach by claiming that social play may take one of many forms, depending on the degree and kind of consensus among players. What appears to be parallel and associative play may be precipitated by a fully cooperative ongoing play relationship. Understanding the quality of a play interaction at a given point in play requires relating the interaction to its antecedents and possible consequences.

The present chapter describes the evolution of play interaction in terms of collaborative construction between play partners. The specific aims of the chapter are twofold: The primary purpose is to demonstrate that social pretend play is a process of negotiation involving children's attempts to reach minimal agreements in order to maintain the play activity. That is, children actively, selectively, and flexibly negotiate play with their partners on the basis of shared knowledge of events and standards of behavior, as well as on the basis of unique personal experience. The second purpose is to show that the quality of negotiations changes in content and form as social pretense evolves and that this process is reflected in different phases of play. In what follows, I will first provide a theoretical framework for the discussion of shared and personal foundations of negotiations. Subsequently, I will review current research findings in terms of developmental patterns in the negotiations that transpire during four phases of social play: (a) becoming a member of a play group; (b) making a transition into the pretend mode; (c) planning and maintaining social pretend play; and (d) terminating pretend play.

COGNITIVE AND AFFECTIVE BASES OF NEGOTIATIONS

Two theories provide a useful framework in understanding differential negotiation strategies in the course of play: Script theory (Nelson & Gruendel, 1981) and affective theory (Fein, 1985; in press) have proffered explanations for how preschool children jointly construct and maintain their play. Script theory leads us to investigate the nature of play texts as an expression of children's developing notions of daily events. In its original conception (Schank & Abelson, 1977), a script is defined as a cognitive structure that represents a person's understanding of events in a familiar context. Stated differently, a script is a well-defined and predictable sequence of behaviors or actions embedded within the course of a routine activity. For example, a grocery-shopping script involves going to the store, picking up groceries, and paying for them, among other things.

Script theory has been applied to the analysis of children's play. Some researchers (e.g., Bretherton, 1984; Nelson & Seidman, 1984) note that children's play is based on scripted familiar events. In order to sustain coherent social play, the play script must be shared by all participants. After children reach an agreement on a play script, that script generates action formats enabling children to engage in enactment of sequenced events (Garvey, 1977; Garvey & Berndt, 1975). Further, once scripts are determined, they allow players to transform familiar events in play. Thus, a scriptual analysis of play reveals the extent to which play is an expression of children's shared knowledge of objects, roles, and events.

Analysis of children's play from an affective viewpoint presents a different picture (Fein, 1985; in press). In this view, pretend play is a representation of the child's inner world in terms of the child's personal and idiosyncratic symbols. A playing child is not motivated to reveal anything about his or her knowledge or perception of events in play, but rather reinterprets and reconstructs experiences that have emotional meaning. According to the affective theory (Fein, 1985), play is an expression of how a child becomes aware of and regulates inner affective life in the presence of others (Piaget, 1962). As such, affective theory states that play is a free-flowing activity with invented themes, unpredictable structure, changing emotional tone, and transformed identities. Play is a symbol system with a personal and affective quality that is not always based on shared knowledge, daily experiences, or sequence of actions.

At first glance, script and affective theories may appear to present two contradictory conceptualizations of play. Script theory focuses on pretend play as an expression of shared knowledge and experience in culturally acceptable terms. Affective theory emphasizes personal and emotional antecedents of what children do in a collaborative fashion during play. However, both views are useful in explaining the unfolding of social pretend play at different levels. I argue that children come simultaneously to play with both their script-based and personal knowledge. Children refer to script knowledge and strategies in becoming part of a play group. However, as play progresses, children discuss the course of their pretend interaction in both scriptual and personal terms. Children's shared knowledge allows them to establish a general framework for their play and provides grounds for the negotiation of play through individual contributions. Thus, script-based knowledge enables children to establish common standards of behavior, allowing for the more free-flowing expression of personal experiences.

BECOMING A PART OF PRETEND PLAY

The first phase of play involves making an entry into the play group. There is a growing body of literature on how children become a part of peer groups (Hartup, 1983). The literature on group entry and play research (e.g., Rubin et al., 1983) has been considered separately with a few notable exceptions (e.g., Schwartzman, 1978) in discussions of peer interaction. However, in order to have a complete understanding of how children's play interaction evolves, communicative processes involved in group entry must be also included as a phase of play.

There is considerable evidence that entering into a play group is not an arbitrary matter. Indeed, anthropological and psychological studies suggest that gaining access to the play group requires a series of negotiations. Further, entering child's negotiations lead to group admittance only if such negotiations are based on a set of scripted communication strategies.

Common and successful strategies that preschoolers follow in seeking admittance to the play group involve implicit and indirect expression of the desire to participate. For example, Corsaro (1979) found that the preponderance of entry strategies in the spontaneous play of 3- and 4-year-olds were nonverbal approaches, verbal or nonverbal production of a variant of the group activity, and nonverbal occupation of the play area. Children who made explicit requests or disrupted the play activity were rejected by the group with no further discussion. However, when children gave implicit and indirect messages of their wish to participate, they were given further opportunities for negotiation even after the initial rejection. Corsaro thus found that, when children use nonintrusive access strategies in sequence, the likelihood of gaining acceptance increases. For example, if children are first rejected after nonverbally approaching the group, they may subsequently be taken into the group if they produce a variant of the activity.

The need for negotiations in order to become a member of the play group becomes more pronounced at older age levels. In a series of studies, Forbes and his coworkers (Forbes, Katz, Paul, & Lubin, 1982; Forbes & Yablick, 1984; Lubin & Forbes, 1984) found that, when entering the play group, 5-year-olds tend more than 7-year-olds to ask disruptive questions or to ignore the responses of others. In contrast, 7-year-olds more frequently observe the play group, offer and receive information about themselves and the group, and make suggestions about activities.

Investigations of peer popularity provide further support for the idea that group entry is a sequential process with well-defined strategies. Popular kindergartners and first graders make group-oriented statements (e.g., "That looks like a fun game you're playing.") when they express their interest in the group, but rejected and neglected children make bids that are predominantly attention getting (e.g., throwing a ball to the table at which the group is playing) and disruptive (e.g., taking away the play group's toys) (Dodge, Schlundt, Schocken, & Delugach, 1983). Group-oriented statements receive positive responses, while disruptive and attention-getting strategies receive negative responses from the group. The findings of Dodge et al. are consistent with those of other investigators (e.g., Dodge, 1983; Putallaz, 1983; Putallaz & Gottman, 1981), showing that popular first, second, and third graders make entry bids consistent with the play group's interest.

It appears that direct requests to enter a play group interrupt the ongoing activity of the group and are subject to rejection. However, nonintrusive approaches open avenues for negotiations rather than demand a response from the play group. It seems that there is a developing and discernible relationship between seeking acceptance and becoming a part of the play group. With age, the entering child becomes increasingly verbal and relevant. However, one crucial aspect of seeking group entry seems to remain the same over the course of development. Regardless of age, to participate in ongoing group play a child must go through a scripted sequence of actions: approach the group without making demands, indirectly express interest in the group activity, and wait for the group response (see Asher, 1983; Garvey, 1984).

INITIATION OF SOCIAL PRETEND PLAY

The second phase in the evolution of social pretense involves making a transition from the nonpretend mode into the pretend mode. Such a transition marks the achievement of agreement between play partners on at least at two levels. First of all, in order to engage in play, the potential participants must reach consensus on the changing states of their interaction from nonplay to play. In the terms of Bateson (1955), the children must be able to "exchange signals which would carry the message 'This is play' " (p. 40). Second and relatedly, the players must agree that actions in play should be interpreted at their representational value and not at their face value. As Bateson states, playing children are aware that "those actions in which we now engage do not denote what these actions for which they stand would denote" (p. 40). For example, when a 4-year-old girl says, "I'm getting married" as she swishes her hips, she is perhaps inviting her partner to play house rather than informing the partner about a serious marriage.

How do children make a transition to the pretend mode once a play group is established? Are there scripted ways of giving the message that the activity is play rather than nonplay? These questions have not been explored extensively in the play literature. However, the existing evidence suggests that preschoolers follow identifiable strategies in moving into the pretend mode of interaction.

Children's initiation of social pretense is similar to their group entry process. In an observational sltudy of 5-year-olds (Genishi, 1983), two strategies of initiating social pretense were identified. The first strategy, start playing, involves immediate initiation of role enactment (e.g., the child produces "Ding dong" sounds as she pretends to knock on an imaginary door). The second strategy, play by regulation, involves discussion of roles before enactment (e.g., the child claims, "I'm the doctor" then asks the partner, "How do you put the apron on?"). The children studied followed the start-playing strategy more than play-by-regulation. Also, start playing was found to be a more successful means of engaging in play than play by regulation. Thus, preschoolers are implicit in telling their partners that they are beginning to pretend (Giffin, 1984). These findings are entirely consistent with those of other researchers (e.g., Göncü & Kessel, 1984; McLoyd, Thomas, & Warren,1984; Stockinger–Forys & McCune–Nicolich, 1984), who report that preschool children between 3 and 5 years of age initiate their play by pretending rather than by explicitly discussing how to play.

A previous study of dyadic play (Göncü, 1983) illustrates how children make the transition to the pretend mode. The following exchange between two 5-year-old boys clearly illustrates that initiation of pretense in preschool play is accomplished without directly commenting on the changing state of interaction. M and E first explore the toys in a playroom. Then M picks up a helmet as E examines a kimono that he finds on the clothes rack.

M — (Puts helmet on and walks toward E, extends arms to the sides, smiles and exlaims) *[I'm] Superman! Who are you?*

E — (As he puts a kimono on, he declares) *Superboy.*

M — *You change into Superman when you grow up, Superboy.*

As evidenced in this example, pretend play begins after one of the players announces his pretend identity. Clearly, E's message [I'm] "Superman! Who are you?" is not a direct invitation to pretense, such as the message "Let's pretend to be superheroes." However, the context and the way in which E declares to be Superman is taken as an invitation to play. In fact, in the ensuing play session the boys engage in an extensive dramatization of superheroes.

Children follow similar procedures in making transitions to the pretend mode after play is interrupted by an unexpected event. According to Schwartzman (1978) and others (e.g., Wolf & Pusch, 1983) children create new themes to incorporate the interrupting event into the ongoing activity. In one example, Schwartzman found that, when one of the children fell on the ground unexpectedly, the other children immediately changed the play theme by making what Schwartzman calls maintenance statements (e.g., "Daddy hurt himself; quick, Mary, bring the bandages," p. 239). In this way, children give the message that they are back in the pretend mode after the interruption.

These findings suggest that initiating social pretense is one type of adjustment to the overtures of a play partner and changing circumstances. Children accomplish this adjustment without openly talking about the incongruencies between their scripts and without disrupting the activity when there are unexpected events. Instead, by giving predominantly nonverbal messages that they want to play, or by talking indirectly about the unexpected events, children express their desire to engage in pretend play. For example, I have observed boys raise their eyebrows, open their eyes widely, stare at a certain point, and breathe deeply as they prepare to "fly" (Göncü, 1983). Those who pretend to be mothers usually talk to their "babies" with a low and soft voice and bend toward the babies in showing their affection (Miller & Garvey,

1984). Finally, girls who get ready for a pretend marriage make sure that they walk graciously in their high heel shoes as they practice the marriage numerous times in front of the mirror. In sum, the unspoken convention seems to involve giving the message "This is play" through facial expressions, changing intonation patterns, and exaggerated movements (Giffin, 1984; Sutton–Smith, 1983).

PLANNING AND EXPANDING SOCIAL PRETEND PLAY

The processes of initiating and planning social pretend play are inextricably connected. Indeed, children may initiate social pretense by expressing their plans. Regardless of the sequence of initiation and planning, however, the planning of social pretense is based on direct and explicit forms of communication. Increasing evidence suggests that preschool children devote a great deal of talk to the joint construction and maintenance of their play (Field, DeStefano, & Koewler, 1982; Göncü & Kessel, 1985; McLoyd, 1980), as evidenced in the following example.

J and A are in the kitchen corner of the preschool playroom. A initiates the play interaction by proposing a plan for a pretend party.

A — *Hey, J, pretend we're gonna have a party tonight.* (Rolls rolling pin on the table)

J — *I know, this, this is the food we're having for the party.* (Puts a piece of playdough in the teapot and places the pot on the stove)

A — *Yeah, yeah, this is the food that we're having for the party tonight. We gotta clean up the room. Or, or nobody or the kids won't want to play. So, clean it up.*

J — *These go here.* (Starts moving toys around)

A — *And this goes here, this goes here, this goes there.* (Stacks blocks up)

A — (Looks around to make sure that the room is clean, then turns to J.) *Come on J, let's go cook.* (Pats J on the back)

J—*Okay.*

A—*Wait! . . . I'm gonna put this over here.* (Puts up a toy)

J—(Starts singing) *Cooking's gonna be good tonight. Put this to cover it.* (Puts a cup on the teapot) *Okay. All done.*

After having prepared the room for the party, the boys engage in extensive planning of cooking for the party. They make "hot dogs" first.

A—(Rolls playdough on the table.)

J—*Yeah, that needs to be rolled. When you get it all the way rolled take it out and put it in the tea- pot. This is rolled down hot dogs.* (Shows a piece of playdough to A and then puts it in a pan)

A—*Here's, here's, a hot dog.* (Gives J a piece of playdough)

Then the children make "cupcakes."

J—*We're gonna make some cup- cakes, too.*

A—I know—that's what I'm making right now.

J—*Okay.*

Finally, they make "chocolate pudding."

J—(Beats playdough with a mixer) *Shchch [Mixing sounds]. Now we need . . .* (Puts mixer on the ta- ble) *This is going to be chocolate pudding.*

A—*Okay.*

Initial planning of the party is now completed.

J—*A, all these things, we're getting ready to go to the party, ain't we?*

*We're gonna have a fun time, ain't
we? We're gonna have a party at
a disco place?*

                                            A — *We're gonna have a party at our
                                               house.*

J — *It'll be fun dancing, won't it?*

The party starts at A's signal.

A — *I'm already through cooking.
Somebody's already here.
"Come in."* (Pretends to open
the door and invites the imaginary guest inside)

Consonant with an interpretation that draws from both script and affective theories, planning in play can be seen as a process of explicit negotiations on the basis of both scripted and personal knowledge. Detailed examinations indicate that the planning process is prefixed by general statements that evoke script-like structures for children's current and ensuing activities. However, once the general content of the play interaction is determined, children make reference to their own personal experiences in determining how play should evolve. For example, a statement such as "Hey, J, pretend that we're goin' to a party tonight" cues the children to determine the general course of action in play as similar to the action in a real party. Simultaneously, the same statement allows each player to talk about personal experiences and concerns (such as cooking, cleaning, and dancing) in the course of such play. In the view presented here, the unfolding of play is dependent upon the degree of consensus reached between play partners regarding possible discrepancies in their understanding of events.

Evidence exists that determination of general play content by evoking scripts is developmentally determined. Children younger than 3 do not make explicit statements in expressing play content (Fein, Moorin, & Enslein, 1982). Instead, they adopt roles and use speech registers in planning their pretend interaction, as evidenced in doll play (Miller & Garvey, 1984). After 3 years of age, however, children express explicitly their desire to engage in particular play episodes. Several researchers have found that, between 3 and 5, children's plan statements establish general scripts for social pretense (Field, DeStefano, & Koewler, 1982; Gearhart, 1979; Göncü & Kessel, 1984; Sachs, Goldman, & Chaille, 1984). This finding is in keeping with the theoretical views (e.g., Nicolich, 1977; Piaget, 1962) that pretend play themes become increasingly collective after 3 years of age.

The second step in the planning of social pretend play involves negotiating the course of action. The fact that children agree on a common play script does not mean that the ensuing play interaction is smooth. Each child's understanding and personal experience regarding the agreed-upon play theme may be different on many grounds. Therefore, it is plausible that, in the most ideal form of play planning, each player expresses his or her own plan, finds out about the partner's plan, and then negotiates a shared plan. In this sense, planning negotiations can be based on personal rather than common knowledge.

Gearhart (1979) provided an empirical evaluation of how children at 3, 5, and 6 years plan dyadic role play in the context of a pretend grocery store. She identified two general steps in children's planning. The first step, prearrangments, involves public announcements of what partners want to play (e.g., "I'm buying the food. Now you take it."). The second step involves negotiation of shared plans. While all the age groups studied consistently announced their play plans, 3-year-olds and most of the 5-year-olds did not seem to consider the possibility that their partners might have their own agenda for play. In contrast, these children informed their partners about procedures for role play. Only 6-year-old children negotiated shared plans by expressing their own play plans first and then compromising such plans according to the experiences and intentions of their play partners.

These findings suggest that there are identifiable developmental patterns in the planning of social pretend play. Before 3 years of age, children begin to play without establishing a shared context for their interactions. Between 3 and 5, children's efforts to reach a mutually acceptable play niche are evidenced in their general plan statements and developing negotiations. During the preschool years, children begin to talk about their personal experiences in terms that are relevant to their play partners. At 6, children openly discuss idiosyncrasies deriving from their personal backgrounds and resolve conflicts in their attempt to develop shared play plans.

One set of questions still remains, however. Why do children choose certain scripts rather than others for their play? How do they determine mutually agreed-upon ways of conducting their play? What criteria do children use in determining the appropriateness of their actions for the ongoing play script? What, in summary terms, are the bases of their negotiations?

These questions are now being explored by researchers espousing the affective theory of play (Fein, 1985; Piaget, 1962). The answer to the question concerning children's choice of scripts comes from Piaget: The novel experiences that are emotionally meaningful to children constitute the background of children's play scripts. According to Piaget (1962), one function of imaginative play is to assimilate to reality. In other words, Piaget regards play as an activity in which the child imposes on the immediate environment and actual experience a structure that is totally under his or her control (Fein, in press). Because of this nature of play, some researchers (e.g., Fein, 1975) have called play a transformational activity. In transforming the environment and actual experience, the child tests his or her mastery over past events and affect associated with it. For example, Fein (in press) claims that play is an arena for the child to use the immediate environment in the way he or she wants to re-create and reconstruct what has happened in the past. In turn, this process of reconstruction helps the child to understand and regulate inner affective life. Such an affective function of play has been explored recently by Field and Reite (1984) in a study of 22- to 60-month old firstborn children's reactions to the arrival of a new sibling. In comparing parent–child play during the mothers' prehospitalization, hospitalization, and post hospitalization, the researchers found that children's aggression and anxiety deriving from the arrival of a sibling were expressed in their play. Following the sibling's birth, decreases took place in the frequency of cooperative play, visual orientation, and suggestions for play themes occurring between the parents and the older child. Also, qualitative analyses revealed that firstborn children pretended that their mothers and siblings were in accidents, thus possibly expressing their frustration at having to share parental affection with a new sibling. This evidence is consistent with theoretical claims that play serves an emotional release function (Piaget, 1962; Vygotsky, 1978) and that play scripts are based on previous personal experience.

How can such a personal experience be a criterion in determining the course of action in social pretense? Corsaro (1983) explored this question in an ethnographic examination of the play of preschool girls. In this study, one of the 3-year-old girls constantly attempted to incorporate a brother theme into an ongoing script dealing with television. This attempt did not receive any response from the other players. In fact, although the given child insisted on pretending to see her brother on the television, the other girls constantly ignored her overtures.

In an interview with the mother, Corsaro found out that the birth of a new baby brother had taken place before the play session was conducted. Indeed, the mother also reported that the girl saw her new sibling on a television monitor at the hospital. Leaving the interpretation of why the older child wanted to pretend that her baby brother was on television, Corsaro concluded that, in order to share an experience with other children in play, a script about which all children are knowledgeable must be found. To Corsaro's conclusion I will also add the point that, once a mutually agreeable play script is established, the players must also find appropriate ways of talking about the affect associated with such a script.

Consider the following exchange between two 5-year-old girls as an example of how, once a play script is evoked, children negotiate their play through the expression of appropriate information and related effect.

M and R are in the kitchen corner of the preschool playroom. As R makes pretend eggs at the table, the following conversation takes place:

M — *Somebody is listening at the door.* (Looks at the door)

R — *Ahh.* (Whispers in M's ear as she pretends to be afraid)

M — (Goes over to the door, braces her back against it) *Want me to call the police?*

R — *Yeah.* (Very quietly)

M — *Lock the door and call the police.* (Makes sure that the door is locked)

R — (Intensely watches M)

M — (Comes to the table and picks up the telephone receiver) *Hello, oh it's, will you get the police?* (She is out of breath) Please come and get him because we live on Southwest Freeway. Will you hurry up and get him? (Pauses) That's all right, okay bye-bye. *That's the police.* (To R) *They live at Southwest by our house. Know what! Remember that one!* . . .

R — *They live up there, right?*

M — *Yeah, remember we went there.* (Acts scared)

R — *Yeah, and there was a widdy fight.*

M — *Yeah, remember, so remember.*

R — *Because that's when we come there they put somebody in jail.*

The episode begins when M evokes a threat script by announcing that somebody is listening at the door. Then both children decide that they should call the police in order to avoid the source of threat, an imaginary person. The episode ends when R mentions that somebody was put in jail. The children's negotiations in this brief exchange reveal information about their script-like knowledge in defending themselves against a potential threat.

Also, such negotiations may express these children's concerns regarding the possibility that their homes may be broken into. Further, it seems that as M cues R by saying, "Remember . . . so remember" she is both probing R to contribute to the developing script and also providing grounds for the expression of fright, an affect embedded within the context of their pretend interaction. The consensus between these children regarding the unfolding of the play event and the feelings associated with it allows them to engage in a sustained sequence of pretend interactions. This example suggests that social pretense requires affective as well as cognitive synchrony between players. It seems that in social pretense the suitability of the individual player's affect to the ongoing pretend theme of the group is a criterion in determining whether such affect should be incorporated into play (Fein, 1985). In order to engage in social pretense, players must reach a consensus not only on how they should represent an event but also on how they feel about it.

In analyzing children's play negotiations, much emphasis has been given to the analysis of scripted event representations (e.g., Bretherton, 1984). Recent examinations consistently show that with increasing age the coherence and communicability of play scripts increase significantly. This is evidenced in the increasing degree of sophistication in children's pretend phone conversations (Garvey & Berndt, 1975), cooking and baking (Nelson & Seidman, 1984), doctor–patient role play (Sachs et al., 1984), and mother–baby role play (Bretherton, 1984; Dunn & Dale, 1984; Miller & Garvey, 1984). These findings collectively indicate that children jointly represent events in their play with an increasing degree of complexity between 3 and 5 years of age. However, it remains to be explored what kind of personal experience and affect are expressed and shared in play. It is not yet known how each player learns to express private and personal matters in ways that are meaningful to other players. In future research, it will be especially informative to focus specifically on the processes by which children express, discuss with others, and change the way they feel about people, events, and objects.

TERMINATION OF SOCIAL PRETEND PLAY

Termination of pretend play is perhaps the least understood phase of social pretense. Studies examining the termination of completed sequences of pretend play report that children terminate play in ways similar to their initiation of pretense. Göncü and Kessel (1985) report that, in the play of 3- and 5-year-olds, less than 1% of the players' total utterances are termination statements (e.g., "I'm not playing in the kitchen anymore."). Termination of pretend play due to disagreements between players has not yet been explored. Although the study of negotiations has gained recent currency in the study of play, it is not known how negotiations may lead to termination. It is, however, plausible to hypothesize that lack of minimal shared knowledge and affect may lead to termination of pretense (Fein, 1985; Garvey & Berndt, 1975; Schwartzman, 1978). The following exchange between two 5-year-old girls illustrates how a play episode can be terminated before it develops.

R — *You're the mother and I'm the mother and we don't have no children* (Holds a ballet tutu)

A — *Yes we do, we're going to get some.* (Putting a hat on) *'Cause we're going to have a baby soon. Only I am because my mommy is going to have a baby soon.* (Very loudly)

R — *Yeah.* (Quietly)

A — *Did you know that?* (Angrily asks the researcher)

Researcher — *Not really.*

A — *Well, she is.* (In a low voice)

This script of mother play was immediately aborted after A declared, "I'm going to play with this [a purse]" following her brief exchange with the researcher. R's desire to play mothers with no children and A's revealing statement that "they are going to have baby" created a conflict. Indeed, A's loud and angry tone seemed to convey the message that, regardless of whether they would have children or not, she was not going to play "mothers." The fact that A's mother was pregnant at the time may reinforce the interpretation that R's suggestion triggered angry emotions from A. The incongruence between girls in the way they felt about playing mothers brought this conversation to an end.

CONCLUSIONS

A complete cycle of social pretend play unfolds in terms of four phases: formation of play groups, transition to the pretend mode, planning and maintaining play, and, finally, terminating play. Children also negotiate with one another in moving from one phase of play to another in the course of pretend interaction.

Although social pretense unfolds in terms of four phases, it is essential to note that not every example of social pretense involves all four phases. Indeed, it is often the case that preschool play groups attempt to maintain themselves without allowing newcomers, thus skipping the first phase (Corsaro, 1979). Furthermore, I do not mean to suggest that the four phases of play occur in a sequential fashion. Not so surprisingly, some of these phases may coincide. For example, preschoolers sometimes make the transition into the pretend mode by expressing their plans or symbolic representations (Göncü & Kessel, 1984). Finally, play can be terminated before it completes its due course. In the event that potential players cannot define a shared pretend theme or disagree regarding the course of action, play may come to an end before it begins.

Regardless of whether the four phases are present or not within a play relationship each phase requires negotiations of a different sort. In the beginning of play, negotiations are based on determining potential players. These negotiations are conducted implicitly, and they lead to a predictable result. If the entering child expresses his or her interest in participating in the group activity in terms of a script common to the preschool peer group, that child will be accepted. Otherwise, he or she will be rejected.

The content and communicative form of negotiations change as play evolves (Kelly–Byrne, 1984). Survival in the play group and maintenance of play depends on the degree of relevance to other players. Unless a minimal degree of shared understanding is assured regarding the choice of events, knowledge about the chosen event, the affect associated with it, and an appropriate way of talking about it, play comes to an end.

Depending upon the degree of shared representation of events (Nelson & Gruendel, 1981), affect (Fein, 1985; in press) and forms of communication (Göncü & Kessel, 1984), children's play interaction may take different forms. For example, if play is based on explicitly communicated familiar events and is devoid of deeply felt personal variations, play interaction may be based on a sequence of actions, as the script theory predicts. However, with an increasing degree of personal involvement and discrepancy regarding the play script and affect, children may seek to develop a mutually acceptable play text. In such an attempt, the proposed scripts may be changed, expanded, transformed, or completely given up. It is at this point that play will be a free-flowing activity, as the affective theory predicts.

Existing findings suggest that the nature of play interaction presents developmental patterns. During infancy, symbolic representations are based on unique personal experiences (See Fein, 1981). However, during the preschool years, children find shared ways of talking about daily events (Nelson & Seidman, 1984) and also use invented themes (Genishi, 1983). Additionally, there is evidence that children's symbolic representations (Watson & Fischer, 1977) and play conversations (Göncü & Kessel, 1984) become increasingly sequential and continuous with age. Thus, it is likely that play becomes more scripted with age, although it retains its personal qualities.

Future research needs to identify developmental changes in the evolution of play interaction. Currently, there is little information available on how children reach agreements with one another as play progresses. The processes by which preschool children initiate, maintain, and terminate play and the cognitive and affective foundations of shared scripts need further investigation. If social pretense is an expression of shared meanings, future studies must determine how children collectively think, feel, and talk about their experiences in play. We need to examine what knowledge and related affect children bring to play, how they talk about such knowledge and affect in play, and, finally, how they change as a result of their play interactions. It stands to reason that dynamic analysis of pretend play will illuminate not only the phenomenon itself, but will also yield information on how much children know about their culture.

REFERENCES

Asher, S.R. (1983). Social competence and peer status: Recent advances and future directions. *Child Development, 54,* 1427–1434.

Bateson, G. (1955). A theory of play and fantasy. *Psychiatric Research Reports, 2,* 39–51.

Bretherton, I. (1984). Representing the social world in symbolic play: Reality and fantasy. In I. Bretherton (Ed.), *Symbolic play* (pp. 1–41). New York: Academic.

Corsaro, W. (1979). "We're friends. Right?": Children's use of access rituals in a nursery school. *Language in Society, 8,* 315–336.

Corsaro, W. (1983). Script recognition, articulation and expansion in children's role play. *Discourse Processes, 6,* 1–19.

Dodge, K.A. (1983). Behavioral antecedents of peer social status. *Child Development, 54,* 1386–1399.

Dodge, K.A., Schlundt, D.C., Schocken, I., & Delugach, J.D. (1983). Social competence and children's sociometric status: The role of peer group entry strategies. *Merrill–Palmer Quarterly, 29,* 309–336.

Dunn, J., & Dale, N. (1984). "I a daddy": 2-year-olds' collaboration in joint pretend play with sibling and with mother. In I. Bretherton (Ed.), *Symbolic play* (pp. 131–158). New York: Academic.

Fein, G. (1975). A transformational analysis of pretending. *Developmental Psychology, 11,* 291–296.

Fein, G. (1981). Pretend play in childhood: An integrative review. *Child Development, 52,* 1095–1118.

Fein, G. (1985). The affective psychology of play. In C.C. Brown & A. Gottfried (Eds.), *Play interactions: The role of play toys and parental involvement in children's development,* (p. 19–28). Skillman, NJ: Johnson & Johnson.

Fein, G. (in press). Pretend play: Creativity and consciousness. In D. Gorlitz & J. Wohlwill (Eds.), *Curiosity, imagination and play: On the development of spontaneous and motivational processes.* Hillsdale, NJ: Erlbaum.

Fein, G., Moorin, E. R., & Enslein, J. (1982). Pretense and peer behavior: An intersectoral analysis. *Human Development, 25,* 392–406.

Field, T., DeStefano, L., & Koewler, J.H., III (1982). Fantasy play of toddlers and preschoolers. *Developmental Psychology, 18,* 503–508.

Field, T., & Reite, M. (1984). Children's responses to separation from mother during the birth of another child. *Child Development, 55,* 1308–1316.

Forbes, D.L., Katz, M.M., Paul, B., & Lubin, D. (1982). Children's plans for joining play: An analysis of structure and function. In D.L. Forbes & M.T. Greenberg (Eds.), *Children's*

124   Göncü

planning strategies (pp. 61–80). San Francisco: Jossey–Bass.
Forbes, D., & Yablick, G. (1984). The organization of dramatic content in children's play. In F. Kessel & A. Göncü (Eds.), *Analyzing children's play dialogues* (pp. 23–36). San Francisco: Jossey–Bass.
Garvey, C. (1977). *Play*. Cambridge, MA: Harvard University Press.
Garvey, C. (1984). *Children's talk*. Cambridge, MA: Harvard University Press.
Garvey, C., & Berndt, R. (1975, August–September). *Organization of pretend play*. Paper presented at the annual meeting of the American Psychological Association, Chicago. (ERIC Document Reproduction Service No. ED 114 891).
Gearhart, M. (1979, March). *Social planning: Role play in a novel situation. Paper presented at the biennial meeting of the Society for Research in Child Development, San Francisco, CA.*
Genishi, C. (1983, April). *Role initiation in the discourse of Mexican-American children's play.* Paper presented at the annual meeting of the American Educational Research Association, Montreal.
Giffin, H. (1984). The coordination of meaning in the creation of a shared make-believe reality. In I. Bretherton (Ed.), *Symbolic play* (pp. 73–100). New York: Academic.
Göncü, A. (1983). *Development of preschoolers' imaginative play: Cognitive and communicative aspects.* Unpublished doctoral dissertation, University of Houston, TX.
Göncü, A. (1984, August). *Can you tell the player from the play: Reflections and conjectures.* Paper presented in the symposium "Interpretive vs. Natural Science View of Symbolic Behavior," F. Kessel (Chair), at the annual meeting of the American Psychological Association, Toronto.
Göncü, A., & Kessel, F. (1984). Children's play: A contextual-functional perspective. In F. Kessel & A. Göncü (Eds.), *Analyzing children's play dialogues* (pp. 5–22). San Francisco: Jossey–Bass.
Göncü, A., & Kessel, F. (1985). Preschoolers' collaborative construction in planning and maintaining imaginative play. Manuscript submitted for publication.
Hartup, W. (1983). Peer relations. In E.M. Hetherington (Ed.), *The handbook of child psychology: Social development* (pp. 103–196). New York: Wiley.
Kelly-Byrne, D. (1984). Text and context: Fabling in a relationship. In F. Kessel & A. Göncü (Eds.), *Analyzing children's play dialogues* (pp. 37–52). San Francisco: Jossey–Bass.
Lubin, D., & Forbes, D.L. (1984). Children's reasoning and peer relations. In B. Rogoff & J. Lave (Eds.), *Everyday cognition* (pp. 220–229). Cambridge, MA: Harvard University Press.
Miller, P., & Garvey C.M. (1984). Mother-baby role play: Its origin in social support. In I. Bretherton (Ed.), *Symbolic play* (pp. 101–130). New York: Academic.
McLoyd, V. (1980). Verbally expressed modes of transformations in the fantasy play of black preschool children. *Child Development, 51,* 1133–1139.
McLoyd, V.C., Thomas, E.A.C., & Warren, D. (1984). The short-term dynamics of social organization in preschool triads. *Child Development, 55,* 1051–1070.
Nelson, K., & Gruendel, J. (1981). Generalized event representations: Basic building blocks of cognitive development. In M. Lamb & A. Brown (Eds.), *Advances in developmental psychology* (pp. 131–158). Hillsdale, NJ: Erlbaum.
Nelson, K., & Seidman, S. (1984). Playing with scripts. In I. Bretherton (Ed.), *Symbolic play* (pp. 45–72). New York: Academic.
Nicolich, L. (1977). Beyond sensori-motor intelligence: Assessment of symbolic maturity through analysis of pretend play. *Merrill-Palmer Quarterly 23,* 89–99.
Parten, M.B. (1932). Social participation among preschool children. *Journal of Abnormal Psychology, 27,* 243–269.
Piaget, J. (1962). *Play, dreams and imitation in childhood.* New York: Norton.

Putallaz, M. (1983). Predicting children's sociometric status from their behavior. *Child Development, 54,* 1417–1426.

Putallaz, M., & Gottman, J.M. (1981). An interactional model of children's entry strategies into peer group. *Child Development, 52,* 986–994.

Rubin, K.H., Fein, G., & Vandenberg, B. (1983). Play. In E.M. Hetherington (Ed.), *The handbook of child psychology: Social development* (pp. 693–774). New York: Wiley.

Rubin, K.H., Maioni, T.L., & Hornung, M. (1976). Free play behaviors in middle and lower class preschoolers: Parten and Piaget revisited. *Child Development, 47,* 414–419.

Rubin, K.H., Watson, K., & Jambor, T. (1978). Free play behaviors in preschool and kindergarten children. *Child Development, 49,* 534–536.

Sachs, J., Goldman, J., & Chaille, C. (1984). Planning in pretend play: Using language to coordinate narrative development. In A.D. Pellegrini & T.D. Yawkey (Eds.), *The development of oral and written language in social contexts* (pp. 119–128). Norwood, NJ: Ablex.

Schank, R., & Abelson, R. (1977). Scripts, plans, goals and understanding. Hillsdale, NJ: Erlbaum.

Schwartzman, H. (1978). *Transformations: The anthropology of children's play.* New York: Plenum.

Stockinger–Forys, S., & McCune–Nicolich, L. (1984). Shared pretend: Sociodramatic play at 3 years of age. In I. Bretherton (Ed.), *Symbolic play* (pp. 159–194). New York: Academic.

Sutton–Smith, B. (1983). Piaget, play and cognition revisited. In W. Overton (Ed.), *The relationship between social and cognitive development* (pp. 229–249). Hillsdale, NJ: Erlbaum.

Wolf, D. (1984, August). *Shared information in play episodes: Beyond a single-minded theory of human activity.* Paper presented in the symposium "Interpretive vs. Natural Science View of Symbolic Behavior," F. Kessel (Chair), at the annual meeting of the American Psychological Association, Toronto.

Wolf, D., & Pusch, J. (1983, April). *The origins of autonomous texts in play boundaries.* Paper presented at the annual meeting of the American Educational Research Association, Montreal.

Vygotsky, L. S. (1978). *Mind in society: The development of higher mental processes.* Cambridge, MA: Harvard University Press.

Watson, M.W., & Fischer, K.W. (1977). A developmental sequence of agent use in late infancy. *Child Development, 48,* 828–836.

AUTHOR NOTES

I am grateful to Barbara Rogoff, Jacqueline Goodnow, Douglas Teti, Kathleen Gilbride, Teresa Ficula, and Jayanthi Mistry for their helpful comments on previous versions of this paper.

The present chapter was presented at the annual meeting of the International Society for the Study of Behavioral Development, Tours, France, 1985, July. Reprint requests should be sent to Artin Göncü, College of Education, University of Illinois at Chicago, Chicago, IL 60680.

7

Children's Humor:
A Cognitive-Developmental
Perspective

Amelia J. Klein

Wheelock College

Children demonstrate their knowledge in a variety of contexts. Cognitive psychologists, who believe that much of what children do reflects their thinking, have extended this concept to the realm of humor.

Like play, humor is of enormous importance to young children. Those who observe preschool children for any period of time conclude that young children find a great many things humorous; preschoolers are generally described as being easily amused. But not all things found humorous by young children are equally amusing to adults. It is perplexing to adults, at times, that children find certain events amusing while adults consider them "silly," "nonsense," or nonhumorous. The opposite also holds true: Young children do not always understand and appreciate "adult" humor. In attempting to understand how children's concepts of humor differ from those of adults, researchers have concluded that the development of humor parallels and is dependent upon the development of cognition.

HUMOR AS A COGNITIVE PROCESS

Structure of Humor

Humor that appeals to older children and adults may take many forms (jokes, riddles, or cartoons), but most forms of humor are based on structural properties believed to be universal (Berlyne, 1969; Jacobs, 1964; McGhee, 1972b; Rothbart, 1976; Shultz, 1972). These properties have been identified as *incongruity* and *resolution* (McGhee, 1979; Rothbart & Pien, 1977; Shultz, 1976; Suls, 1972).

Incongruity in humor results when there is a discrepancy between the punch line and the body of the joke (Nerhardt, 1976; Shultz, 1972) and a violation of expectancies (Shultz, 1972, 1976). Jokes, cartoons, and riddles are deliberately constructed to trick or deceive the listener and to generate incongruity (Eysenck, 1942; Suls, 1977). The following riddle is an example:

How do you catch a rabbit?
Stand behind a bush and make a noise like a carrot.

(Gerler, 1975, p. 6)

In attempting to answer the initial question in the above riddle, the recipient of humor probably would contemplate a rabbit trap or some other device used to lure wild animals into captivity. Upon hearing the punch line, the recipient's expectations would not be confirmed, and a brief period of cognitive uncertainty would exist. As Shultz (1976) summarizes: "Incongruity is usually defined as a conflict between what is expected and what actually occurs in the joke. It is a concept which accounts well for the most obvious structural feature of jokes, the surprisingness of the punch line" (p. 12).

Humor is not experienced until the recipient discovers a comic relationship between the body and the punch line of the joke. This final phase of the humor experience has been described as resolution (Berlyne, 1969; Jones, 1970; Pien & Rothbart, 1976; Shultz, 1972; Suls, 1972). Shultz (1976) defines resolution as a "more subtle aspect of jokes which renders incongruity meaningful or appropriate by resolving or explaining it" (p. 13). Within this context, humor is defined as a problem-solving task in which a solution is required before a joke is fully understood.

Process of Humor

The process of resolving comic incongruity has been examined in relation to the structure of humor and the cognitive status of the recipient. Both approaches assume that appreciation of intended humor is contingent upon comprehension of the joking relationship and the underlying cognitive concepts on which the humor is based.

In the first stage of humor processing, the recipient must identify an incongruity in the structure of the joke. Consider the following example:

Mother Mouse was taking her children for a stroll. Suddenly a large cat appeared in their path. Mother Mouse shouted, "Bow-wow-wow!" and the cat scurried away. "You see, my children," Mother Mouse said, "it pays to learn a second language" (Gerler, 1975, p. 12)

In the above story, humor is based on violations of the concepts of "people," "animals," and "human language." A basic notion of people includes such human activities as taking a walk, speaking to other people, or learning a second language. In the context of the joke, these human abilities have been attributed to animals. In addition, various onomatopoeic terms (imitation of natural sounds) are classified as different language systems ("bow-wow-wow" versus "squeak squeak"). In order to identify these comic incongruities, a child first must have acquired the basic underlying concepts of people, animals, and language systems.

In the second stage of humor processing, the recipient must engage in resolving the major discrepant elements discovered in the first stage. In order to establish a joking relationship between the above incongruities, the recipient must playfully assume that the frightened cat was led to believe the mouse was really a dog because it could bark and that "barking" represents a foreign language. When this joking relationship is discovered, the intended humor is understood, appreciated, and usually followed by smiling or laughter. The humor experience culminates in the resolution of discrepant elements.

Shultz (1970/1971, 1972) contends that the recipient of humor must employ specific strategies in order to resolve cognitive incongruity. Resolution types commonly used in children's cartoons are shared characteristic (incongruous elements share some crucial characteristic), physical analysis (physical factors establish a joking relationship), motivational conflict (characters involved in humorous situations exhibit conflicting motive states), participant misapprehension (incongruity is explained in light of some mistake or misunderstanding), and personal deviance (one of the characters displays eccentric behavior).

Suls (1972, 1977) has proposed that the recipients of humor engage in another type of problem-solving strategy. He states that the recipient tries to identify a *cognitive rule* that reconciles the incongruous elements within the confines of the joke. Suls explains that, by retrieving a cognitive rule and determining how it has been violated, the recipient is able to consider the parts of the joke "congruous." The following example used by Suls (1972) demonstrates rule violation:

Fat Ethel sat down at the lunch counter and ordered a whole fruit cake.

"Shall I cut it into four or eight pieces?" said the waitress.

"Four," said Ethel, "I'm on a diet." (p. 83)

The cognitive violation the recipient must detect in order to appreciate the above humor is substitution of the rule of number value (increase in number constitutes an increase in the total amount) for the rule of conservation of quantity (the quantity of the cake remains the same whether cut into four or eight pieces).

According to cognitive theorists, humor is constructed by the individual

(Fry & Allen, 1975; Keith-Spiegel, 1972; McGhee, 1979; Wilson, 1927). The process of humor in this view can be defined as "the interaction between the recipient and some structural aspect of the stimulus . . . . [During the course of] assimilating the humor stimulus into existing cognitive structures, a joke, cartoon, or riddle can be understood and appreciated" (Goldstein, Harman, McGhee, & Karasik, 1975, p. 60). Existing cognitive structures therefore play a major role in the comprehension of humor. As will be discussed in the next section, cognitive theorists also have delineated the origins and development of humor as it relates to the development of thought.

HUMOR AND THE DEVELOPMENTAL PROCESS

Humor has been viewed as a developmental process that reflects underlying cognitive changes. Theorists have attempted to define the general cognitive prerequisites for incongruity humor and the stage at which young children first are capable of understanding comic incongruity.

Origins of Incongruity Humor

Most humor theorists agree that humor is a response to the perception of incongruity. Theorists disagree, however, in their explanation of the cognitive processing necessary for a humor response to occur and in their interpretation of the onset of incongruity humor within the developmental sequence (McGhee, 1979; Pien & Rothbart, 1980; Shultz, 1976).

Shultz (1976) has proposed that appreciation of pure incongruity in humor coincides with the onset of preoperational thought at about 18 to 24 months of age. During this period, the child becomes capable of symbolic representation (Piaget, 1962), which Shultz defines as "self-constructed incongruity." When children pretend that an object is something other than what it really is, they create "an incongruous relationship between the object and the scheme applied to it; the object is inappropriate to the scheme and the scheme is inappropriate to the object" (Shultz, 1976, p. 23).

The cognitive prerequisites for incongruity humor, according to Shultz, are the acquisition of symbolic play capacities and the ability to create and perceive incongruity as a violation of expectancies. Since they cannot form specific expectations about future events, presymbolic children are capable of perceiving only novel or expected events as humorous (Shultz, 1976). Shultz and others have proposed that an incongruous stimulus is cognitively more complex than one that is novel (Charlesworth, 1969; Rothbart, 1977) and is beyond the cognitive capacity of infants.

Like Shultz, McGhee (1971a, 1977c, 1979) has proposed that the onset of humor occurs with the acquisition of symbolic play capacities. However,

McGhee (1971a) argues that incongruities do not become associated with humor until the child has acquired the capacity for conceptual thought. The acquisition of concepts occurs as the child's thought becomes more stabilized through a process Piaget termed "equilibration." Others have described this period of stabilized thought as "cognitive mastery" (Jones, 1970; Kris, 1938; McGhee, 1974a, 1977c; Wolfenstein, 1953, 1954). Because the child's mental structures are more stable, "there are fewer situations that will throw the new structures into disequilibrium" (Brainerd, 1978, p. 20). What results is a sense of confidence in one's own knowledge about objects or events. It is this sense of confidence or conceptual mastery that allows the child to view a humor situation as inappropriate and a "play on reality" (McGhee, 1979). McGhee (1972a, 1979) has termed this playful mental disposition "fantasy-assimilation." During fantasy-assimilation, the individual incorporates a humorous event without accommodating or altering existing cognitive structures to fit the novel aspects of the stimulus. Comic incongruity, like play, is experienced at the "assimilatory stage of cognitive functioning" (Piaget, 1962). According to McGhee, fantasy-asssimilation plays a key role in generating the humor response. Young children develop the ability to fantasy-assimilate events around the third year of life.

McGhee (1974a) has stated that Shultz's prerequisites for incongruity humor are insufficient for a true humor response, arguing that, prior to conceptual mastery, children who have developed representational thought may experience a primitive form of humor "simply by assimilating an event into the 'wrong' schema" (p. 722). According to McGhee's view, incongruity must not simply be perceived as misexpected or different from prior experience, but must also be viewed as inconsistent with previously developed mental structures. McGhee further asserts that the cognitive prerequisites for incongruity humor are the acquisition of symbolic play capacities, conceptual thought and cognitive mastery, and the ability to contemplate incongruity as fantasy. Other theorists disagree with McGhee's position. Pien & Rothbart (1980) have argued that the capacity for symbolic play as defined by Piaget (1962), Shultz (1976), and McGhee (1979) is not necessary for the humor experience to occur.

In contrast to Shultz, Pien and Rothbart (1980) argue that children are able to recognize incongruities as violations of expectations prior to the acquisition of symbolic play capacities. The authors point out, however, that the "cognitive expectancies" of infants are qualitatively different from those of young children in later stages of development (see Bower, 1971; Bower, Broughton, & Moore, 1971). Because expectancies are related to (and are the result of) previously formed mental structures such as object concept, it is reasonable to assume that the mode of incongruity enjoyed by infants plays an important role in facilitating the humor response. For example, infants might show pleasure when encountering a familiar object that has been altered but would not respond to incongruities based on violations of language rules. The authors argue that infants and young children may find real-life incongruities, such as a person wearing a large hat or unusual clothing, amusing. Pien and Rothbart therefore conclude that all that is necessary for experiencing humor is the ability to detect incongruities per se and the capacity for "playful" or ludic (Piaget, 1962) assimilation of incongruous events.

The major theorists cited above differ in their operational definitions of comic incongruity and in their interpretations of the degree of comprehension necessary for a child to perceive an incongruous event as humorous. Theorists have recently argued that a uniform definition of incongruity is necessary for researchers investigating the development of humor (McGhee & Chapman, 1980; Nerhardt, 1977). As McGhee and Chapman summarize:

> Play, incongruity and arousal fluctuations undoubtedly have a central role in the earliest forms of humor, just as they are central to humor generally (Berlyne, 1972). The main issue for future consideration seems to be whether these must be combined with the make-believe activities which accompany symbolic thinking to produce humor, or whether they are sufficient to produce humor perceptions before the onset of symbolic capacities . . . . In speculating about the origins of humor, we might benefit by distinguishing between misexpected and unexpected events, between active and passive expectations regarding an event, and between the child's level of awareness of the unusualness of the event. (1980, p. 283–284)

In further determining a young child's "level of awareness," humor comprehension may be defined as the resolution of incongruous elements (i.e., the discovery of a joking relationship between those elements). Developmental changes concerning the nature of incongruity and the resolution process will be reviewed in the following section.

Stages of Humor Development

Comic incongruity may be presented visually, verbally, or in both modes and may be represented by objects, behavior, social norms, or language. Linguistic ambiguity has received the most attention in studies of children's humor. One reason may be that language is predominantly a rule-oriented system and is most suitable for humor based on the violation of rules (Shultz & Robillard, 1980). The most common forms of linguistic ambiguity (corresponding to the child's developing metalinguistic knowledge) are lexical, phonological, syntactical surface structure, and deep structure. The type of incongruity found humorous by children of various ages corresponds to general trends in cognitive development. McGhee (1979) has delineated the development of incongruity-based humor from its origins early in the second year to its more abstract form in middle childhood. Each of his developmental stages corresponds to a specific cognitive acquisition as defined by Piaget (1950, 1952, 1962).

According to McGhee's model, the first forms of humor responses occur during the second year of life, with the onset of symbolic play. During this stage, children playfully manipulate objects and images with actions known to be at odds with reality. Piaget (1962) provides an example of early humor in describing his daughter's playful manipulation of concrete symbols:

> [Jacqueline] saw a cloth whose fringed edges vaguely recalled those of her pillow; she seized it, held a fold of it in her right hand, sucked the thumb of the same hand and lay down on her side, laughing hard. She kept here eyes open, but blinked from time to time as if she were alluding to closed eyes. (p. 96)

Jacqueline, at the age of 15 months, thus experienced pleasure by playfully using a cloth as if it were a pillow.

The ability to perceive action–object–image discrepancy as humorous is based on the capacity to engage in playful forms of activity and to recognize the inappropriateness of an action toward an object. Incongruities at this stage are exclusively self-initiated. McGhee suggests that very young children are much more confident that an incongruity is improbable when they themselves construct it. It is only when children have gained sufficient cognitive mastery over their environment that they may fantasy-assimilate humorous stimuli introduced by others.

Toward the end of the second year, the child's developing language competency is employed in a second form of symbolic play, the inaccurate labeling of objects and events. During this stage, humor is perceived in the absence of action toward objects and is based primarily on verbal statements or inaccurate descriptions of actions or objects. Humorous incongruities characteristic of this stage consist of inappropriate naming of objects readily understood by the child (e.g., calling a dog a cat or a boy a girl). Such image manipulation and name-change humor usually lasts through the late preschool years. By the age of 3, the child begins to shown an interest in humor introduced by others in the presence of strong play signals. As a result, humor experiences become socially oriented as children share them with their peers or adults.

During the third stage of humor development, McGhee suggests that the child's capacity for incongruity humor is enhanced with the development of conceptual thought. Between the ages of 3 and 4, the child begins to organize objects and events sharing key characteristics. Incongruity-based humor occurs when one or more aspects of a given class concept are violated. According to McGhee, distortions of essential characteristics (such as a cat with two heads or no fur) are likely to be funny, whereas distortions of nonessential characteristics (such as a cat with red fur) are not found humorous. This stage in the development of humor continues until the age of 6 or 7. Humor at this level may be experienced visually (seeing a cat with two heads in a cartoon), verbally (hearing another person describe a cat with two heads), or mentally (imagining to oneself a cat with two heads).

During the first three stages of humor development, the child appreciates explicit humor based on concrete situations. The child's social knowledge can now be applied to humorous situations in which the child's concepts of social norms are violated. Children at this stage may laugh at a person who speaks a foreign language, eats with chopsticks, or wears a native costume. Linguistic humor found appealing by young children is primarily based on phonological ambiguity (Shultz & Pilon, 1973). Children during this stage may spend countless hours creating nonsense words (e.g., "itsy," "bitsy," "witsy," "mitsy," etc.) and develop an appreciation of books based on phonological variation, such as Dr. Seuss's *Cat in the hat*.

McGhee suggests that the fourth stage of humor occurs with the onset of concrete-operational thinking around the age of 7 or 8, when children perceive humor in abstract expectancy violations based on the relationships between events rather than in end states or outcomes of event. A new source of incongruity is found in behavioral inconsistencies and linguistic ambiguity. Humor based on logical and illogical thought patterns appears to develop sequentially during this stage. Logical incongruity is recognized first in the form of ambiguous word meanings and next in humor containing nonlexical (conceptual) ambiguities based on behavioral expectations (Whitt & Prentice, 1977).

Behavioral inconsistencies represent a more abstract form of incongruity and are not based on visual discrepancies. Rather, these inconsistencies are based on hidden or implied meanings that require concrete-operational thought processes. McGhee (1979) cites the following joke as an example of humor based on behavioral incongruity:

"Well, I see you have a new dog. I thought you didn't like dogs."

"I don't! But my mother bought a lot of dog soap on sale, so we had to get a dog to use it up." (p. 77)

In order to discover the implied meaning contained in the above humor, the child must be capable of mentally inverting ideas, a process Piaget (1969) has defined as "reversibility." Reversibility also is required in order to comprehend humor based on linguistic ambiguity. The following joke, made famous by W. C. Fields, illustrates this point:

Announcer: "Mr. Fields, do you believe in clubs for young people?
W. C. Fields: "Only when kindness fails."

(Shultz, 1976, p. 13)

In order to understand the joking relationship, the recipient of humor must understand and compare the double meaning of the word "club," a process that requires a "mental replay" and reorganization of events.

The ability to detect various forms of linguistic ambiguity is mastered between the ages of 6 and 12. Following mastery of phonological ambiguity around the age of 12, lexical ambiguity and finally surface structure and deep structure ambiguities are understood (Kessel, 1970; Shultz & Horibe, 1974; Shultz & Pilon, 1973).

RESEARCH ON YOUNG CHILDREN'S HUMOR

Laughter-provoking Situations

To date, researchers have focused primarily on young children's humor preferences, their responses to various humor stimuli (e.g., smiling and laughter), and their productive humor. Prior to 1970, studies of preschool children lacked any theoretical orientation. Most early studies were designed to explore conditions that would elicit laughter. Nursery school children were most often observed during unstructured, "free play" sessions. Researchers found that mirth responses occurred frequently during children's motor activity (Ames, 1949; Ding & Jersild, 1932; Enders, 1927; Gregg, 1928; Jones, 1926; Kenderdine, 1931; St. Clair–Hester, 1924; Wilson, 1931). A more recent study of preschool children found that gross physical-motor actions precipitated glee in group situations (Sherman, 1975).

Several other factors listed as prominent in the study of young children's laughter included the following observations:

1. Preschool children exhibited wide individual differences in their humor preferences (Brackett, 1934).
2. Surprise was found to be an important ingredient of humor most enjoyed by young children (Justin, 1932; St. Clair–Hester, 1924).
3. As children grew older, they laughed at a greater variety of things (Justin, 1932, Perl, 1933), particularly instances involving pretense, recognition of oddities, teasing, recognition of one's own predicament, violation of convention, plays on words, and absurdities (Wilson, 1931).

Two studies of preschool children have provided a more global account of early forms of humor than those discussed above. Justin (1932), in an unusual experimental study, presented 3- through 6-year-old children with a variety of laughter-provoking situations. The author found that laughter was associated with

1. Surprise (such as encountering an empty jack-in-the-box),
2. Superiority and degradation (such as seeing the experimenter deliberately missing a chair and falling on the floor),
3. Incongruity and contrast situations (for example, viewing a picture of a cow playing a piano),
4. Social smiling (as might occur when observing the experimenter discuss the weather while smiling and laughing),
5. Relief from strain (as might be experienced after having been asked to walk on a line drawn on the floor while holding a small umbrella and a potato on a spoon),
6. Play situations (such as having the experimenter read nonsense verse and introduce various toys).

One important finding of the Justin study was that, as age increased, incongruity played a more important role in preschool children's humor. This finding supports the hypothesis of McGhee (1974a, 1977b, 1979), who has proposed that the development of conceptual thought capacities allows children to perceive a greater number of things as incongruous and potentially humorous.

In a more recent study designed to assess the relation of humor episodes to ongoing play activities, Groch (1974) found that humor is not a unitary trait but rather has multiple aspects. Three- and 4-year-old subjects most often produced their own humor in the form of silliness, clowning, teasing, word play, and absurdity during unstructured activities such as free play. Responsive humor predominated during more structured activities (such as cooking or story experience), which provided unexpected or surprising events. Both the Justin and Groch studies of preschool children's humor preferences support the findings of others who suggest that young children are very playful and find a great many things humorous in association with their past experiences and their present play activities. These studies also suggest that preschool children enjoy comic incongruities that are physically represented in some way, a position taken by McGhee (1971b, 1971c, 1972a, 1979).

Humor and Cognitive Mastery

A preliminary condition to experiencing the comic is cognitive mastery (Jones, 1970; Kris, 1938; McGhee, 1974a, 1977a; Wolfenstein, 1953, 1954). Cognitive mastery is attained when an individual's knowledge has become stable enough so that it can be used simply for fun (Athey, 1977). The greater the level of knowledge or cognitive mastery of the concepts underlying the humorous situation, the greater the probability of fantasy-assimilation (McGhee, 1972a, 1977b). Cognitive mastery results in confidence about the improbability or impossibility of the humorous events occurring as depicted.

Drawing upon Piagetian concepts to assess the cognitive status of the humor recipient, researchers have investigated qualitative changes in children's problem-solving abilities. This approach has allowed researchers to predict a child's potential for understanding humor based on violations of these concepts. For example, Rothbart (1976) presented 4½- to 6-year-olds with a demonstration of Piagetian conservation of liquid quantity and told them that they were about to see a trick. Younger nonconservers of liquid quantity actually believed a trick was performed by the experimenter when water poured from a short, wide jar into a tall, thin jar appeared to "turn a little water into a lot of water." Results indicated that nonconservers showed greater appreciation because their expectations were not met. In a test designed to match stimulus to schema, McGhee (1976) presented jokes to children in first through fifth grades. The humor depicted was derived from violation of conservation of mass and weight principles. Results indicated a curvilinear relationship between appreciation of humor and level of development of conservation skills.

Using more composite measures, McGhee (1971a, 1971c) initiated a series of studies in order to investigate the cognitive antecedents of humor. Operational thought and the ability to give interpretive (as opposed to descriptive) explanations of humor were found to be an important factor for 7-year-old boys in comprehending incongruity (as opposed to novelty) humor. Novelty humor consisted of physically discrepant events, whereas incongruity humor was based on violations occurring at an abstract, nonperceptual level. McGhee concluded that the ability to explain more abstract incongruity depends upon the use of logic and reversible thought capacities. Younger, preoperational subjects had difficulty in decentering from perceptual characteristics of cartoons and gave more descriptive explanations. In other studies, the acquisition of concrete-operational thought also was found to be related to children's ability to detect hidden meanings of ambiguity (Shultz & Bloom, 1976) and the ability to create a joking relationship (McGhee, 1974b).

Several researchers have investigated the structure and content of humor preferred by children. Wolfenstein (1953, 1954) suggested that the types of jokes told by schoolchildren were associated with their knowledge of the structure of various forms of humor. She found that, around age 6, children were able to retell jokes accurately, including essential structural components of the joke format. Park (1972) also investigated children's humor preferences. Kindergarten through eighth-grade subjects told their favorite riddles, which then were analyzed according to a Piagetian framework. The author concluded that riddles were cognitive structures by which children organize their environment in terms of causal, logical, and psychological relations. Like Wolfenstein's subjects, children progressed from a precursor stage of creating riddles to representing traditional forms. A similar stage was described by Sutton–Smith (1976) in a study of riddles collected from first- and second-grade children. "Preriddles," accounting for a third of the jokes told by the subjects, consisted of pure incongruity (i.e., a puzzling question with an arbitrary, unresolvable answer).

Developmental differences were noted in a study of children's humor preferences conducted by Athey (1977). Ninety percent of the humor contributed by 5-year-olds consisted of incongruous movement, established images, and the location and use of objects. The author concluded that these were schemes that had been sufficiently well assimilated by this age group. Older children presented more complex riddles and puns, which required multiple classification skills in order to be resolved. Humor development also was linked to broader areas of personality development.

The relationship between level of moral development (Piaget, 1932) and children's appreciation of humor based on intentional or unintentional damaging outcomes was examined by McGhee (1974c). The results indicated that, while "heteronomous" children found stories with highly damaging outcomes funny, "autonomous" children appreciated these stories only when the damage occurred unintentionally. Moral development (as outlined by Kohlberg, 1963, 1968) was related to children's explanations of humor (Sheppard, 1977). Development shifts emerged as 8- to 16-year-old children progressed from a "pre-explanatory" level, to statements of rule based on simple recognition of incongruity, to a universal interpretation of events. Other studies of young children have shown that sex-role mastery (McGhee & Grodzitsky, 1973; Wolfenstein, 1954) and degree of self-concept (Petry, 1978) were associated with variations in the comprehension of incongruity humor.

Mastery played an important role in creative humor in a study of 2- to 5½-year-old children. Garvey (1977) examined the language play of preschoolers as they interacted with their peers. Children engaged in verbal play by distorting normal articulation (such as trying to speak with their lips spread apart or speaking in a squeaky voice). Other variations of speech play involved the repetition and variation of newly learned language structures, phonological properties of nonsense syllables and words, and sentence patterns. Garvey concluded that "as soon as a child has learned how something is supposed to be, then turning it upside down or distorting it in some way becomes a source of fun" (p. 38).

The cognitive-developmental studies presented in this section indicate that a high level of mastery over the cognitive elements constituting a humorous situation are essential for the comprehension and appreciation of humor. Studies also have shown that Piagetian concepts provide both theoretical direction and a systematic approach in assessing the cognitive characteristics of humor stimuli and the developmental level of children participating in humor experiments.

Moderately Novel Humor Stimuli

Researchers have applied the theories of Piaget and White to explain motivational and affective aspects of humor. Piaget (1952) postulated that moderately novel stimuli generate maximal intellectual stimulation. White (1959) introduced the "effectance motivation" concept, arguing that organisms are intrinsically motivated and seek to master their environment, deriving immense pleasure from their competence. In humor, this pleasure is derived when incongruous elements are resolved. Applying White's theory to their studies, Zigler, Levine, and Gould (1966, 1967) found that pleasure was greatest when humor stimuli were congruent with the cognitive structure of the child (i.e., when humor was in the moderately difficult range of the difficulty dimension). They referred to this process as the "cognitive congruency principle." McGhee and Eisele (1973) presented Piagetian tasks to subjects functioning at various levels of operational thought. First-grade conservers of mass gave the highest appreciation ratings; a drop in scores occurred for nonconservers and more cognitively advanced subjects.

McGhee (1976) further refined the cognitive congruency model. The author presented humor stimuli based upon violations of specific conceptual acquisitions to children varying in the degree of (or the length of time since) acquisition of conservation and class inclusion concepts. Results indicated that appreciation of related humor was greatest soon after concepts were acquired. Nonconservers and subjects who had mastered the concepts several years earlier showed less appreciation. Another study found correlations between mastery of more general thought capacities (such as acquisition of concrete operational thought) and children's heightened enjoyment of humor (Whitt & Prentice, 1977).

Studies of the cognitive congruency principle presented in this section provide evidence that humor depends on cognitive mastery "new enough to be interesting; old enough to be firm" (Blos, 1979). Findings of these studies emphasize the importance of establishing a "match" (Hunt, 1965) between the cognitive resources of the subject and the cognitive demand features of the humor stimulus (Brodzinsky & Rightmyer, 1980; McGhee, 1977a; Shultz & Zigler, 1970).

Structural Aspects of Humor

Researchers have examined incongruity and resolution components separately to determine their role in young children's comprehension of humor. In one of his earlier studies, Shultz (1970/1971, 1972) found that, when grade-school children were unable to discover the critical incongruity in cartoon humor, they invented one and attempted to resolve it, thus supporting the hypothesis that a recipient of humor must consider both incongruity and resolution information in order to appreciate a joke fully.

Researchers have tested children's appreciation of either incongruity or resolution by eliminating one of these components from the humorous content. Shultz (1974) and Shultz and Horibe (1974) presented 6-, 8-, 10-, and 12-year-old children with a series of original, resolution-removed, and incongruity-removed riddles and verbal jokes based on linguistic ambiguity. Results indicated that children under the age of 8 did not appreciate the resolvable nature of incongruities. The author considered these findings evidence for a developmental theory of humor, suggesting an early stage involving comprehension of pure, unresolved incongruity followed by a later stage of preference for resolvable incongruity. A similar study conducted by Sutton–Smith (1976) found that appreciation of pure incongruity shifted to appreciation of resolvable incongruity between the ages of 6 and 8. None of the studies cited above, however, provided a cognitive match for younger subjects, as had been proposed by McGhee (1977a) and others.

In the studies he reported, Shultz (1974) found that 6-year-old children had particular difficulty detecting hidden meanings in humorous content. The ability to detect hidden meanings requires previous knowledge that words have dual meanings. In addition, the ability to comprehend double meanings is dependent upon "the capacity to reverse ideas, simultaneously entertain contradictory hypotheses, and understand the implied" (Blos, 1979, p. 39), capacities that do not appear until the age of 7 or 8. Studies have shown that humor based on hidden meanings is not comprehended or appreciated until the onset of concrete-operational thought, which occurs well beyond the preschool years. Shultz's conclusion that young children are not capable of resolving comic incongruity may be applicable only to certain types of humor. Other researchers have found evidence that young children are capable of resolving humorous incongruity when the joking relationship is dependent upon cognitive structures already acquired by the children.

Pien and Rothbart (1976) have argued that Shultz could not generalize his findings because his studies were based on language-based humor and did not use developmentally appropriate stimulus materials. These investigators tested Shultz's model by using explicit content that did not require comprehension of linguistic ambiguity. Specifically, they presented preschool subjects with both original and resolution-removed versions of cartoons selected from children's books and magazines. One cartoon was presented showing several dogs sitting in front of a television set. This cartoon was followed by two captions: "A boy says to his mother, 'They're watching a dog food commercial' " (original version) or "A boy says to his mother, 'They're watching a commercial' " (resolution-removed version). The 4- and 5-year-old subjects found the original version funnier than the resolution-removed version. The authors concluded that preschool children are capable of appreciating resolvable incongruities when presented with "simple, age appropriate stimulus materials" (p. 968).

In a study of children's comprehension and appreciation of storybook humor, Klein (1983) found that kindergarten children fully comprehended and were able to resolve comic incongruity, thus supporting the hypothesis of Pien and Rothbart (1976). The issue of how and whether preschool children utilize the resolvable aspects of incongruity humor needs further examination. Studies designed to match the cognitive characteristics of humor stimuli with the developmental level of the recipient would help researchers examine young children's understanding of the joking relationship.

SUMMARY OF RELATED RESEARCH

Researchers have attempted to demonstrate the role of cognitive factors in children's comprehension and appreciation of humor. There is general agreement that cognitive level is significantly related to the child's understanding of the joking relationship. Empirical studies of children's humor suggest that

1. The degree of cognitive conflict generated by a humor stimulus plays an important role in determining the child's comprehension and appreciation of humor in both early and late stages of development.
2. Humor preferred by young children is concrete and based on the violations of expectancies that children have developed through previous experience. Logic plays no part in preoperational children's understanding of incongruity humor.
3. Humor parallels general patterns of language development. Humor based on more advanced forms of linguistic ambiguity is beyond the cognitive capacity of preschool children.
4. The element of surprise is an important ingredient in young children's humor.
5. Children enjoy humor that is consistent with their intellectual capacities. In order to match stimulus to schema, researchers have established a link between the cognitive resources of the subject and the cognitive demand features of the humor stimulus.
6. Piagetian concepts provide a theoretical framework in which to assess the developmental level of the recipient of humor and to create humor stimuli based on violations of concepts.
7. Incongruity and resolution are essential components of the humor of adults and older children. Recent studies have shown that children as young as 4 or 5 appreciate the resolvable aspects of incongruity humor when the humor stimulus is appropriate to their age and developmental level.

The classroom is an ideal environment in which to observe children's spontaneous humor experiences. Groch's (1974) naturalistic study of preschool children provides a model for studies of productive and responsive humor. In further exploring young children's perceptions of "funniness" (i.e., comic incongruity), researchers need to investigate the types of physical incongruities found humorous by preschoolers, particularly in the context of ongoing play activities. Future studies might address the following questions: How do children create humorous incongruities at the water play area, the block area, or at a sandbox? What do young children understand about the structure of humor (i.e., does their humor include the elements of incongruity, surprise, or resolution)? and, How soon after mastery do young children use their knowledge to create comic incongruity?

Analysis of humor created by adults for young children also warrants further investigation. Studies designed to evaluate the appropriateness of humor in children's literature and television programs would provide further information about the importance of a "cognitive match" between the cognitive demand features of the humor stimulus and the cognitive status of the humor recipient.

HUMOR AND EARLY CHILDHOOD EDUCATION

Laughter is a common sound in early childhood classrooms and places where young children congregate. Research suggests that humorous episodes enjoyed or created by children are not simply a source of entertainment but are also a means of cognitive stimulation. Research further suggests that the origins and development of humor are contingent upon the development of general thought processes.

The role that humor plays in the development process is receiving increasing attention. Child development textbooks and reference books now include discussions of cognitive humor (e.g., Fein, 1978, Schickedanz, Schickedanz, & Forsyth, 1982; Wolman, 1977). Entire books review general humor research (e.g., Chapman & Foot, 1976, 1977; Goldstein & McGhee, 1972; McGhee & Goldstein, 1983) as well as research on young children's humor comprehension and appreciation (e.g., McGhee, 1979; McGhee & Chapman, 1980). Humor as a cognitive process is also of interest to early childhood educators. Four areas that warrant further investigation are (a) humor as a motivating factor, (b) the value of humor in spontaneous play activities, (c) the role of humor in the learning process, and (d) the types of humor most appreciated by young children.

Humor as a Motivating Factor

Humor has been observed to be an important factor in children's preferences. When young children are given a choice in selecting humorous versus nonhumorous materials, they more often choose the former. Illustrating this point, researchers found that humor was a highly appealing factor in children's selection of television programs (Brown & Bryant, 1983; Zillman & Bryant, 1983). Producers of children's educational programs (such as "Sesame Street" and the "Electric Company") have employed humor in order to facilitate learning. Researchers have suggested that the interspersion of humorous stimuli in television programs increases children's attention span and intellectual curiosity (Zillman & Bryant, 1983).

Humor also was found to be a motivating factor in children's storybook preferences (e.g., Abrahamson, 1980; Fleischman, 1976; Tibetts, 1973). One explanation for the highly appealing nature of humorous stimuli is the element of surprise. In both humorous television programs and humorous literature, children are presented with moderately novel misexpected situations. Theorists have stated that misexpected events (i.e., those events that violate expectancies) generate greater epistemic curiosity (Charlesworth, 1969; Rothbart, 1977, Shultz, 1976). The appealing nature of humor might also be explained in light of the fact that young children have a lower threshold for humor and tend to be play-oriented — in other words, they are more often in a playful frame of mind than older children and adults (McGhee, 1979). Humor, as a form of play, provides children opportunities for playful manipulation of the real world.

During the course of sharing humor with young children, adults attempt to test children's comprehension of humorous material. This task may affect motivation if children are asked to be objective about the humorous episodes they enjoy. For example, children do not experience any problems responding when asked, "What's so funny?" However, studies have shown that young children cannot explain *why* a particular humorous stimulus is funny. Interpreting humorous content is difficult because the limited language competencies and analytical skills of young children prevent them from explaining the basis for humor (McGhee, 1971a, 1971b, 1974b, 1977a; Pien & Rothbart, 1976). Requiring the child to analyze humorous content may decrease the child's motivation by creating a less "playful" atmosphere.

Humor and Spontaneous Play

Humor has been defined as a form of play behavior (Berlyne, 1969; McGhee, 1979, 1983). The capacity to engage in playful behavior (and humor is considered a highly pleasurable form of play) develops naturally; it is not something that is "taught." Adults who guide children's learning can facilitate humor production by creating a nonthreatening environment where playful forms of behavior are encouraged and by providing children with opportunities to construct (or encounter) incongruities during the course of their daily activities. Adults who are receptive to humor enjoyed by young children and who themselves are humorous create an atmosphere conducive to experimentation and discovery.

During the course of "playing" (e.g., make-believe play), children create incongruities they know to be at odds with reality. A similar situation occurs when children create humorous incongruities. Objects, images, or words are deliberately distorted in violation of concepts or social rules (e.g., creating nonsense words). Children find the creation of comic incongruities pleasurable after they have mastered the underlying concepts and rules that are the basis for incongruity. Humor production therefore can be viewed as a means of exercising and adapting to newly acquired knowledge. In humor, pleasure is derived from the child's understanding of the impossibility or the absurdity of the comic incongruity.

Children generate comic incongruities during dramatic play episodes, painting sessions, or puppet shows. Misexpected, incongruous situations are encountered during ongoing classroom activities, such as storytelling or cooking sessions. Adults can provide further opportunities for children to encounter incongruous situations by structuring activities that deliberately introduce misexpected events. For example, young children who are given cornstarch in place of flour to mix with water, or in another experiment are given various sizes of wires with which to blow bubbles, are quite surprised and delighted at the results.

Role of Humor in the Learning Process

Humor is believed to facilitate learning in the following ways:

1. Humor is a form of play for young children and is a natural medium through which they can expand their understanding of the world.
2. Humor is highly pleasurable and is associated with cognitive mastery.
3. Humor provides children with problem-solving situations. In the context of a joke, riddle, humorous story, or cartoon, children must resolve incongruity in order to establish a joking relationship.
4. Humor promotes divergent thinking, a characteristic of creativity; in order to establish a joking relationship, the child must discover or create unique associations among ideas.
5. Humor provides the child with an opportunity to learn rules. Humor has a basic structure that children discover when "playing jokes" on others (humor is based on the element of surprise) or telling riddles (a punch line is logically related to the body of the joke).

These guidelines are easily applied to classroom activities. Teachers may provide a variety of humorous storybooks for reading activities. These may include traditional story structures as well as poetry. In order to introduce young children to more structured forms of humor, teachers might present simple books of jokes, riddles, and cartoons that contain the elements of incongruity and resolution. Although younger children will not master these formats until the age of 7 or 8, they become interested in jokes and riddles because their older brothers, sisters, or friends are interested in them. Exposing children to more advanced forms of humor allows them to learn about the structure and rules for humor (e.g., a joke contains a body and the punch line and both are logically related within the context of a joke).

Types of Humor Appropriate for Young Children

Children exhibit preferences for humor that reflect their developmental levels. For example, an interest in riddles appears between the ages of 6 and 8. It is during this period that operational thought processes are acquired and allow the child to reverse ideas mentally. Preoperational children (i.e., preschoolers) would not enjoy or be capable of understanding riddles. Similarly, jokes that contain double meanings (puns) or implied meanings (based on illogical behavior) would not be comprehended by young children.

Research has shown that young children are perceptually oriented and enjoy concrete humor. Much of the humor portrayed in children's television programs is based on physical incongruities. However, more sophisticated forms of humor also appear on children's programs, perhaps to appeal to a wider audience, including adults. These forms may be too complex to be cognitively challenging to young viewers. Children's literature also contains a wide range of humorous material. Books that emphasize more complex forms of linguistic ambiguity or illogical behavior are more appropriate for children who are at the concrete-operational level of development. For example, *Amelia Bedelia* (by Peggy Parish) is a story about a girl who takes things literally when she reads a recipe book and is told to "dress a turkey." Young children may laugh at the sight of a turkey wearing a dress but are likely to fail to understand the character's inability to consider several interpretations of the term "dress." In *The man who didn't wash his dishes* (by Phyllis Krasilovsky), a gentleman creates problems by refusing to wash his dishes. The man substitutes other available kitchen utensils, such as flowerpots and ashtrays, until he eventually exhausts his household supplies. He solves his dilemma by taking all his "dirty dishes" outside on a rainy day and resolves never to postpone his daily chores again. Preschoolers usually do not appreciate the man's eccentric behavior or take his actions seriously.

Books depicting physical incongruities are more appealing to preschoolers. In the story *Where can an elephant hide?* (by David McPhail) an elephant tries to avoid being detected by two approaching hunters by imitating the behavior of various jungle animals—a tiger, monkey, and a baboon—then by covering itself with parrot feathers. This story, not surprisingly, was a favorite choice of young children in a national survey conducted by the International Reading Association (1980).

Adults who select or create humorous materials for children can play an important role in selecting humor that is developmentally appropriate for younger recipients. By assessing the developmental level of children and the cognitive content of humorous stimuli, adults can develop guidelines for the selection of books, television programs, and other sources of humorous incongruity. Adults can judge the appropriateness of humor stimuli by the mirth response of the recipient; children, like adults, appreciate what they understand. Although the manifestation of humor is the same for recipients of all ages, the underlying thought processes *are* qualitatively different.

REFERENCES

Abrahamson, R.F. (1980). An analysis of children's favorite picture storybooks. *Reading Teacher, 34,* 167-170.
Ames, L.B. (1949). Development of interpersonal smiling responses in the preschool years. *Journal of Genetic Psychology, 74,* 273-291.
Athey, C. (1977). Humor in children related to Piaget's theory of intellectual development. In A.J. Chapman & H.C. Foot (Eds.), *It's a funny thing, humour* (pp. 215-218). Oxford, England: Pergamon Press.
Berlyne, D.E. (1969). Laughter, humor and play. In G. Lindzey & E. Aronson (Eds.), *The handbook of social psychology* (Vol. 3, pp. 795-852). Reading, MA: Addison-Wesley.
Berlyne, D.E. (1972). Humor and its kin. In J.H. Goldstein & P.E. McGhee (Eds.), *The psychology of humor* (pp. 43-60). New York: Academic Press.
Blos, J.W. (1979). Getting it: The first notch of the funny bone. *School Library Journal, 25,*(9), 38-39.
Bower, T.G.R. (1971). The object in the world of the infant. *Scientific American, 225,* 30-38.
Bower, T.G.R., Broughton, J.M., & Moore, M.K. (1971). The development of the object concept as manifested by changes in the tracking behavior of infants between 7 and 20 weeks of age. *Journal of Experimental Child Psychology, 11,* 182-193.
Brackett, C.W. (1934). Laughing and crying of preschool children. *Child Development Monographs,* No. 14.
Brainerd, C.J. (1977). Feedback, rule knowledge, and conservation learning. *Child Development, 48,* 404-411.
Brodzinsky, D.M., & Rightmyer, J. (1980). Individual differences in children's humor development. In P. McGhee & A. Chapman (Eds.), *Children's humor* (pp. 181-212). Chichester, England: Wiley.
Brown, D., & Bryant, J. (1983). Humor in the mass media. In P.E. McGhee & J.H. Goldstein (Eds.), *Handbook of humor research* (Vol. 2, pp. 143-172). New York: Springer-Verlag.
Chapman, A.J., & Foot, H.C. (1976). *Humor and laughter: Theory, research and applications.* London: Wiley.
Chapman, A.J., & Foot, H.C. (1977). *It's a funny thing, humour.* Oxford, England: Pergamon Press.
Charlesworth, W.R. (1969). The role of surprise in cognitive development. In D. Elkind & J.H. Flavell (Eds.), *Studies in cognitive development* (pp. 257-314). New York: Oxford University Press.
Ding, G.F., & Jersild, A.L. (1932). A study of the laughing and smiling of preschool children. *Journal of Genetic Psychology, 40,* 452-472.
Enders, A.C. (1927). A study of the laughter of the preschool child in the Merrill-Palmer nursery school. *Papers of the Michigan Academy of Science, Arts and Letters, 8,* 341-356.

Eysenck, H.J. (1942). Appreciation of humor: An experimental and theoretical study. *British Journal of Psychology, 32,* 295–309.

Fein, G.G. (1978). *Child development.* Englewood Cliffs, NJ: Prentice–Hall.

Fleischman, S. (1976). Laughter and children's literature. *Claremont Reading Conference Yearbook, 40,* 88–92.

Fry, W.F., & Allen, N. (1975). *Make'em laugh.* Palo Alto, CA: Science and Behavior Books.

Garvey, C. (1977). Play with language and speech. In C. Mitchell–Kernan & E. Tripp (Eds.), *Child discourse* (pp. 27–47). New York: Academic Press.

Gerler, B. (1975). *Riddles, jokes and other funny things.* New York: Western Publishing.

Goldstein, J.H., Harman, J., McGhee, P.E., & Karasik, R. (1975). Test of an information-processing model of humor: Physiological response changes during problem- and riddle-solving. *Journal of General Psychology, 92,* 59–68.

Goldstein, J.H., & McGhee, P.E. (Eds.) (1972). *The psychology of humor.* New York: Academic Press.

Gregg, A. (1928). *An observational study of humor in three-year-olds.* Unpublished master's thesis, Columbia University, New York.

Groch, A.S. (1974). Joking and the appreciation of humor in nursery school children. *Child Development, 45,* 1098–1102.

Horgan, D. (1981). Learning to tell jokes: A case study of metalinguistic abilities. *Journal of Child Language, 8,* 217–224.

Hunt, J. McV. (1965). Intrinsic motivation and its role in psychological development in D. Levine (Ed.), *Nebraska symposium on motivation* (pp. 189–282). Lincoln: University of Nebraska Press.

International Reading Association (1980). Children's choices for 1980. *Reading Teacher, 34,* 37–56.

Jacobs, M. (1964). *Pattern in cultural anthropology.* Homewood, IL: Dorsey Press.

Jones, J.M. (1970). Cognitive factors in the appreciation of humor: A theoretical and experimental analysis (Doctoral dissertation, Yale University, 1970). *Dissertation Abstracts International, 31,* 3038A. (University Microfilms No. 70-25,287).

Jones, M.C. (1926). The development of early behavior patterns in young children. *Pedagogical Seminary, 33,* 537–585.

Justin, F. (1932). A genetic study of laughter-provoking stimuli. *Child Development, 3,* 114–136.

Keith–Speigel, P. (1972). Early conceptions of humor: Varieties and issues. In J.J. Goldstein & P.E. McGhee (Eds.), *The psychology of humor* (pp. 3–39). New York: Academic Press.

Kenderdine, M. (1931). Laughter in the preschool child. *Child Development, 2,* 228–230.

Kessel, F.S. (1970). The role of syntax in children's comprehension from ages six to twelve. *Monographs of the Society for Research in Child Development, 35* (6, Serial No. 139).

Klein, A. (1983). Concept development in relation to humor comprehension and humor appreciation in kindergarten children (Doctoral dissertation, Boston University, 1983). *Dissertation Abstracts International, 43,* 3808A. (University Microfilms No. DA 8309728).

Kohlberg, L. (1963). The development of children's orientations toward a moral order: I. Sequence in the development of moral thought. *Vita Humana, 6,* 11.

Kohlberg, L. (1968). Stage and sequence: The cognitive-developmental approach to socialization. In D. Goslin (Ed.), *Handbook of socialization theory and research* (pp. 347–480). Chicago: Rand–McNally.

Kris, E. (1938). Ego development and the comic. *International Journal of Psychoanalysis, 19,* 77–90.

McGhee, P.E. (1971a). Cognitive development and children's comprehension of humor. *Child Development, 42,* 123–138.

McGhee, P.E. (1971b). Development of the humor response: A review of the literature. *Psychological Bulletin, 76,* 328–348.

McGhee, P.E. (1971c). The role of operational thinking in children's comprehension and appreciation of humor. *Child Development, 42,* 733–744.

McGhee, P.E. (1972a). On the cognitive origins of incongruity humor: Fantasy assimilation versus reality assimilation. In J.H. Goldstein & P.E. McGhee (Eds.), *The psychology of humor* (pp. 61–80). New York: Academic Press.

McGhee, P.E. (1972b). Methodological and theoretical considerations for a cross-cultural investigation of children's humor. *International Journal of Psychology, 7,* 13–21.

McGhee, P.E. (1974a). Cognitive mastery and children's humor. *Psychological Bulletin, 81,* 721–730.

McGhee, P.E. (1974b). Development of children's ability to create the joking relationship. *Child Development, 45,* 552–556.

McGhee, P.E. (1974c). Moral development and children's appreciation of humor. *Developmental Psychology, 10,* 519–525.

McGhee, P.E. (1976). Children's appreciation of humor: A test of the cognitive congruency principle. *Child Development, 47,* 420–426.

McGhee, P.E. (1977a). Children's humor: A review of current research trends. In A.J. Chapman & H.C. Foot (Eds.), *It's a funny thing, humour* (pp. 199–209). Oxford, England: Pergamon Press.

McGhee, P.E. (1977b). Humor development in children. In. B. Wolman (Ed.), *International encyclopedia of psychiatry, psychology, psychoanalysis and neurology* (Vol. 5, pp. 443–444). New York: Van Nostrand Reinhold.

McGhee, P.E. (1977c). A model of the origins and early development on incongruity-based humor. In A.J. Chapman & H.C. Foot (Eds.), *It's a funny thing, humour* (pp. 27–36). Oxford, England: Pergamon Press.

McGhee, P.E. (1979). *Humor: Its origin and development.* San Francisco: W.H. Freeman.

McGhee, P.E. (1983). Humor development: Toward a life span approach. In P. E. McGhee & J.H. Goldstein (Eds.), *Handbook of humor research* (Vol. 1, pp. 109–134). New York: Springer–Verlag.

McGhee, P.E., & Chapman, A.J. (1980). *Children's humor.* Chichester, England: Wiley.

McGhee, P.E., & Eisele, J. (1973). Operational thinking, cognitive challenge, and children's appreciation of humor. Unpublished manuscript. (Cited in P.E. McGhee, Cognitive mastery and children's humor. *Psychological Bulletin,* 1974, *81,* 721–730.

McGhee, P.E., & Goldstein, J.H. (Eds.) (1983). *Handbook of humor research* (Vols. 1,2). New York: Springer–Verlag.

McGhee, P.E., & Grodzitsky, P. (1973). Sex role identification and humor among preschool children. *Journal of Psychology, 84,* 189–193.

Nerhardt, G. (1976). Incongruity and funniness: Towards a new descriptive model. In A.J. Chapman & H.C. Foot (Eds.), *Humour and laughter: Theory, research and applications* (p. 55–62). London: Wiley.

Nerhardt, G. (1977). Operationalization of incongruity in humor research: A critique and suggestions. In A.J. Chapman & H.C. Foot (Eds.), *It's a funny thing, humourf* (pp. 47–51). Oxford, England: Pergamon Press.

Park, R.R. (1972). An investigation of riddles of children, ages five through fourteen, using Piaget derived definitions (Doctoral dissertation, Columbia University, 1972). *Dissertation Abstracts International, 33,* 905A–906A. (University Microfilms No. 72–23, 711)

Perl, R.E. (1933). A review of experiments on humor. *Psychological Bulletin, 30,* 752–763.

Petry, A.K. (1978). *Young children's response to three types of humor.* Unpublished doctoral dissertation, University of Connecticut, Storrs.

Piaget, J. (1932). *Moral judgment of the child.* New York: Harcourt Brace.

Piaget, J. (1950). *Psychology of intelligence.* London: Routledge & Kegan Paul.

Piaget, J. (1952). *The origins of intelligence in children.* New York: International Universities Press.

Piaget, J. (1962). *Play, dreams and imitation in childhood. New York: Norton.*

Piaget, J. (1969). *Judgment and reasoning in the child.* London: Routledge & Kegan Paul.

Pien, D., & Rothbart, M.K. (1976). Incongruity and resolution in children's humor: A reexamination. *Child Development, 47,* 966–971.

Pien, D, & Rothbart, M.K. (1980). Incongruity, humor, play and self-regulation of arousal in young children. In P.E. McGhee & A.J. Chapman (Eds.), *Children's humour* (pp. 1–26). Chichester, England: Wiley.

Rothbart, M.K. (1976). Incongruity, problem-solving and laughter. In A.J. Chapman & H.C. Foot (Eds.), *Humor and laughter: Theory, research and applications* (pp. 37–54). London: Wiley.

Rothbart, M.K. (1977). Psychological approaches to the study of humor. In A.J. Chapman & H.C. Foot (Eds.), *It's a funny thing, humour* (pp. 87–94). Oxford, England: Pergamon Press.

Rothbart, M.K., & Pien, D. (1977). Elephants and marshmallows: A theoretical synthesis of incongruity-resolution and arousal theories of humor. In A.J. Chapman & H.C. Foot (Eds.), *It's a funny thing, humour* (pp. 37–40). Oxford, England: Pergamon Press.

St. Clair–Hester, M. (1924). *Variations in the search for humor according to age and mental condition.* Unpublished master's thesis, Columbia University, New York.

Schickedanz, J.A., Schickedanz, D., & Forsyth, P.D. (1982). *Toward understanding children.* Boston: Little, Brown.

Sheppard, A. (1977). Developmental levels in explanations of humour from childhood to late adolescence. In. A.J. Chapman & H.C. Foot (Eds.), *It's a funny thing, humour* (pp. 225–228). Oxford, England: Pergamon Press.

Sherman, L.W. (1975). An ecological study of glee in small groups of preschool children. *Child Development, 46,* 53–61.

Shultz, T.R. (1971). Cognitive factors in children's appreciation of cartoons: Incongruity and its resolution (Doctoral dissertation, Yale University, 1970). *Dissertation Abstracts International, 32,* 544B. (University Microfilms No. 71-16, 849)

Shultz, T.R. (1972). The role of incongruity and resolution in children's appreciation of cartoon humor. *Journal of Experimental Child Psychology, 13,* 456–477.

Shultz, T.R. (1974). Development of the appreciation of riddles. *Child Development, 45,* 100–105.

Shultz, T.R. (1976). A cognitive-developmental analysis of humor. In A.H. Chapman & H.C. Foot (Eds.), *Humour and laughter: Theory, research and application* (pp. 11–36). London: Wiley.

Shultz, T.R., & Bloom, L. (1976). Concrete operational thought and the appreciation of verbal jokes. Cited in T.R. Schultz, A cognitive-developmental analysis of humor. In A.J. Chapman & H.C. Foot (Eds.), *Humour and laughter: Theory, research and application,* pp. 11–36. London: Wiley.

Shultz, T.R., & Horibe, F. (1974). Development of the appreciation of verbal jokes. *Developmental Psychology, 10,* 13–20.

Shultz, T.R., & Pilon, R. (1973). Development of the ability to detect linguistic ambiguity. *Child Development, 44,* 728–733.

Shultz, T.R., & Robillard, J. (1980). The development of linguistic humour in children: Incongruity through rule violation. In P.E. McGhee & A.J. Chapman (Eds.), *Children's humour* (pp. 59–90). Chichester, England: Wiley.

Shultz, T.R., & Zigler, E. (1970). Emotional concomitants of visual mastery in infants: The effects of stimulus movement on smiling and vocalizing. *Journal of Experimental Child Psychology, 10,* 390–402.

Suls, J.M. (1972). A two-stage model for the appreciation of jokes and cartoons: An information-processing analysis. In J.H. Goldstein & P.E. McGhee (Eds.), *The psychology of humor* (pp. 81–100). New York: Academic Press.

Suls, J.M. (1977). Cognitive and disparagement theories of humor: A theoretical and empirical synthesis. In A.J. Chapman & H.C. Foot (Eds.), *It's a funny thing, humour* (pp. 41–45). Oxford, England: Pergamon Press.

Sutton-Smith, B. (1976). A developmental structural account of riddles. In B. Kirschenblatt-Gimblett (Ed.), *Speech play: Research and resources for studying linguistic creativity* (pp. 111–119). Philadelphia: University of Pennsylvania Press.

Tibbets, S. (1973). What's so funny? Humor in children's literature. *California Journal of Educational Research, 24*(1), 42–46.

White, R.W. (1959). Motivation reconsidered: The concept of competence. *Psychological Review, 66,* 297–333.

Whitt, J.K., & Prentice, N.M. (1977). Cognitive processes in the development of children's enjoyment and comprehension of joking riddles. *Developmental Psychology, 13,* 129–136.

Wilson, C.O. (1931). *A study of laughter situations among young children.* Unpublished doctoral dissertation, University of Nebraska, Lincoln.

Wilson, K.M. (1927). Sense of humor. *Contemporary Review, 131,* 628–633.

Wolfenstein, M. (1953). Children's understanding of jokes. *Psychoanalytic Study of the Child, 8,* 162–173.

Wolfenstein, M. (1954). *Children's humor: A psychological analysis.* Glencoe, IL: Free Press.

Wolman, B. (Ed.). (1977). *International encyclopedia of psychiatry, psychology, psychoanalysis and neurology* (Vol. 5). New York: Van Nostrand Reinhold.

Zigler, E., Levine, J., & Gould, L. (1966). Cognitive processes in the development of children's appreciation of humor. *Child Development, 37,* 507–518.

Zigler, E., Levine, J., & Gould, L. (1967). Cognitive challenge as a factor in children's humor appreciation. *Journal of Personality and Social Psychology, 6,* 332–336.

Zillman, D., & Bryant, J. (1983). Uses and effects of humor in educational ventures. In P.E. McGhee & J.H. Goldstein (Eds.), *Handbook of humor research* (Vol. 2, pp. 173–193). New York: Springer-Verlag.

The ERIC System and ERIC/EECE

ERIC, the largest education data base in the world, is funded by the Office of Educational Research and Improvement of the United States Department of Education. Each month, abstracts and bibliographical information for more than 1,200 documents and 1,500 journal articles on all phases of education are entered into the ERIC data base by the 16 clearinghouses that make up the ERIC system.

Each clearinghouse is responsible for acquiring and processing research reports, program descriptions, curriculum guides, and other documents related to a specific area in education. For example, the ERIC Clearinghouse on Elementary and Early Childhood Education (ERIC/EECE) deals specifically with information on the cognitive, physical, emotional, and social development and education of children from birth through early adolescence.

Like other clearinghouses, ERIC/EECE also publishes topical papers, bibliographies, information digests, bulletins, and resource lists for teachers, parents, administrators, researchers, and policymakers. In addition, staff members respond to requests for information related to elementary and early childhood education.

Information in the ERIC data base can be retrieved by computer search or by using published indexes. Abstracts and bibliographical information are listed in two monthly publications: *Resources in Education (RIE)* and *Current Index to Journals in Education (CIJE)*. The complete text of most ERIC documents announced in RIE can be read on microfiche in ERIC microfiche collections available in more than 700 libraries and information centers. In addition, most of these documents can be ordered in paper copy and/or microfiche from the ERIC Document Reproduction Service, 3900 Wheeler Avenue, Alexandria, VA 22304 (Telephone: 800/227-3742).

CIJE provides access to journal articles, which may be read in the periodicals in which they were originally published. Selected reprints are also available from University Microfilms International (UMI) Article Clearinghouse, 300 North Zeeb Road, Ann Arbor, MI 48106 (Telephone: 800/732-0616).

For complete searching and ordering details, consult the pages of RIE or CIJE. For more information about the ERIC system and about ERIC/EECE, contact ERIC/EECE Information Services, University of Illinois, 805 West Pennsylvania Avenue, Urbana, IL 61801 (Telephone: 217/333-1386).

The ERIC Clearinghouses

ADULT, CAREER, AND
  VOCATIONAL EDUCATION
Ohio State University
National Center for Research in
  Vocational Education
1960 Kenny Road
Columbus, OH 43210
  (614) 486-3655

COUNSELING AND
  PERSONNEL SERVICES
University of Michigan
School of Education, Room 2108
Ann Arbor, MI 48109-1259
  (313) 764-9492

EDUCATIONAL
  MANAGEMENT
University of Oregon
1787 Agate Street
Eugene, OR 97403
  (503) 686-5043

ELEMENTARY AND EARLY
  CHILDHOOD EDUCATION
University of Illinois
805 W. Pennsylvania Avenue
Urbana, IL 61801
  (217) 333-1386

HANDICAPPED AND GIFTED
  CHILDREN
Council for Exceptional Children
1920 Association Drive
Reston, VA 22091
  (703) 620-3660

HIGHER EDUCATION
George Washington University
One Dupont Circle N.W., Suite 630
Washington, DC 20036
  (202) 296-2597

INFORMATION RESOURCES
Syracuse University
School of Education
Huntington Hall, Room 030
Syracuse, NY 13210
  (315) 423-3640

JUNIOR COLLEGES
University of California at Los
  Angeles
Mathematical Sciences Building,
  Room 8118
405 Hilgard Avenue
Los Angeles, CA 90024
  (213) 825-3931

LANGUAGES AND
  LINGUISTICS
Center for Applied Linguistics
1118 22nd Street, N.W.
Washington, DC 20037
  (202) 429-9292

READING AND
  COMMUNICATION SKILLS
National Council of Teachers of
  English
1111 Kenyon Road
Urbana, IL 61801
  (217) 328-3870

RURAL EDUCATION AND
  SMALL SCHOOLS
New Mexico State University
Box 3AP
Las Cruces, NM 88003
  (505) 646-2623

SCIENCE, MATHEMATICS,
  AND ENVIRONMENTAL
  EDUCATION
Ohio State University
1200 Chambers Road, Room 310
Columbus, OH 43212
  (614) 422-6717

SOCIAL STUDIES/SOCIAL
  SCIENCE EDUCATION
Indiana University
Social Studies Development Center
2805 E. 10th Street
Bloomington, IN 47405
  (812) 335-3838

TEACHER EDUCATION
One Dupont Circle, N.W., Suite 610
Washington, DC 20036
  (202) 293-2450

TESTS, MEASUREMENT, AND
  EVALUATION
Educational Testing Service
Rosedale Road
Princeton, NJ 08541
  (609) 734-5176

URBAN EDUCATION
Teachers College, Columbia
  University
Institute for Urban and Minority
  Education
Box 40
525 W. 120th Street
New York, NY 10027
  (212) 678-3433